CULTURE OF LOVE

Cultivating a Positive and
Transformational
Organizational Culture

Luvelle Brown

First Edition
ISBN: 9781732478107
Editing: Wandah Gibbs Ed. D.

Manufactured in the United States

WGW Publishing Inc., Rochester, NY

For my parents, Robert and Lucille Brown, who provided me with the structure, support, and love needed to achieve.

FOREWARD

Controversies. Conflicts. Tensions. Protests. This was the community Dr. Luvelle Brown walked into as an inexperienced and untested superintendent. He and his family were relocating from another state. At 36-years-old, he was one of the youngest superintendents in any state. And he was welcomed into his new community with editorial lines that included, "Please, please, don't tell us you bent over backward to hire this guy just because he's black." Success in this new position was going to be an uphill struggle.

Upon arrival, Luvelle quickly began focusing on a shift of culture – *a culture of love*. He began holding listening sessions and hosting commendation ceremonies. He was present at school plays, modified sporting events, step shows, and orchestra concerts. Luvelle was modeling that a culture of love meant more … more time together; more time sharing; more caring.

Seven years since beginning as a new superintendent, the data in the district is impressive.

Graduations rates for traditionally underserved students have significantly increased. Suspension rates for all students have significantly decreased. And a recent budget vote passed with over 80% approval. This success is the result of a significant shift in organizational culture. And the results of this hard work may help explain the awards and accolades: New York State Superintendent of the Year and National School Boards Association 20-to-Watch or TrustEd's Top 20 Education Thought Leaders.

While talking about love may seem harmless for organizations, as a scholar of Dr. Martin Luther King Jr., I know otherwise. Shoved and shunned. Hit and spat upon. Arrested and assaulted. This is the experience of some when talking about the radical idea of leading with love. And yet, the transformative possibilities of a culture of love make this work the most important work we can do.

Luvelle is still leading an organization that experiences significant conflict and in a community, that is continually working through controversies with serious consequences for children. The question becomes how does a community regularly engage in controversial issues that often tear communities apart? The answer, again, is more.

Luvelle believes a culture of love requires organizations to *more* actively seek out many of the most controversial topics. As he has stated, a culture of love helps us shift so-called controversies into opportunities for learning conversations.

If we are going to learn together, we also need to read and reflect together. We are fortunate that this book explores how to cultivate a culture of love and more.

-Sean Eversley Bradwell, PhD
Ithaca, NY

PREFACE

What you will find in this book:

I hope this book sparks your thinking regardless of your current level of leadership. Each of us is associated with a group of people. Connections to church, work, political organizations, and educational institutions are significant aspects of our lives. Within any group, we have the capacity to lead. Our leadership can positively or negatively impact an organization's culture. We can significantly influence the establishment of a common mental model and inspire people to work toward a collective goal. This book provides a framework for self-reflection and action steps on your personal and professional leadership journey.

My leadership has had an impact on multiple organizations, however, the focus of this book is primarily on my experiences while serving as the Ithaca City School District (ICSD) Superintendent of Schools in Ithaca, NY. During my tenure there, quantitative and qualitative student achievement shifts in the ICSD highlight a remarkable story of transformation. In collaboration with an amazing community, we developed a healthy and collaborative organizational culture as well. This culture will live on for future generations of young people who come through the school doors.

The practices described in this book can be adapted to any organization and community. Hopefully, my leadership experiences and lessons learned will impact your approach to customer service, community building, and your organizations' continuous improvement efforts.

Who is this book for?

While primarily focused on education, I write this book for all who desire to cultivate a positive culture in any organization. Anyone striving to be a great leader can benefit from the culture development process described in this book. Along with garnering a better understanding of organizational change, those reading will gain insight on shifting personal behaviors as well.

A leader is not predicated on a title, but instead on a way of thinking, working, and living. Organizations need innovative and committed leaders as technological advances, political, and social changes alter our global community and economy. This book is for bold leaders who are not afraid to risk losing their job. Those reading this book must feel a sense of urgency in meeting the needs of young people and others they are serving.

While courageous direction is needed today, those leading must cultivate support, understanding, and relationships along the way. I wrote this book for servant leaders who recognize that their commitment to communities and organizations is larger than their personal ego and aspirations. Humble leaders can take lessons from this book on how to build support and coalitions that survive the inevitable challenges associated with significant change efforts.

It is my hope that this book inspires people to reflect on their views and behaviors. Together, we can build new knowledge, strengthen communities, and support our next generation of change agents. I am honored to be on this journey with you!

TABLE OF CONTENTS

CHAPTER ONE

CULTURE EATS STRATEGY FOR BREAKFAST

On January 26, 2011, I stood on stage in Ithaca, NY awaiting more than 1,400 school district employees and guests to arrive for my first presentation as superintendent of schools. To date, being new in town, I had only met a few of the many people I would need to forge working relationships with. Today was the first time I would lay eyes on my colleagues, the people I would be serving. Everything was in place on the stage and my keynote address was all set to begin when I realized the auditorium was still nearly empty.

Nervous, I wondered if I should proceed on time,

> *A leader is not predicated on a title, but instead on a way of thinking, working, and living.*
> *#CultureofLove*

though only a fraction of the anticipated attendees had arrived. Puzzled, I questioned if perhaps an incorrect start time had been listed in the announcement. Surely, folks wouldn't be late for an opportunity to hear from the first new superintendent in 16 years!

Or could the empty room symbolize and echo sentiments shared by the editors of the local newspaper? The Ithaca Times had published a scathing editorial addressed to the board of education which stated, "Please, please don't tell us you bent over backward to hire this guy just because he's black." And, "What we don't want is an ambitious go-getter who's going to go get another job in a higher paying district after a couple of years in Ithaca. This move doesn't do it." Were people boycotting my arrival before they'd even met me?

As I pondered all this, at exactly 10 minutes past the scheduled start time, I noticed a single line of teachers entering the room. They were all dressed in black. Hundreds of others followed marching silently to their seats sending a clear message they were not happy with the state of the school district. The tension was palpable and it was also clear they were unimpressed by their *new* leader.

I stood in silence at the front of the auditorium and wondered if I could perhaps return to my old job in Virginia and forget about working in this new place. However, as I made eye contact with folks in the audience, I heard my mother's calming voice. A few months earlier when informing my parents of my plans to leave the community where we had spent our entire lives, I expected them to make attempts at convincing me otherwise. Instead, my mother stated, "Ships are safest in harbor, but they are made to sail." The challenges ahead of me were daunting, but nothing I couldn't handle.

I ditched my prepared speech as I wondered what I should say to this capacity crowd. I felt the need to begin by validating folks' perspectives and feelings. I eventually broke the silence with, "Good morning, team. I know you are hurting, and I am here to share my thinking about how to stop the pain." My next sentence has been repeated often and has been at the core of continuous improvement efforts. I declared, "Culture Eats Strategy for Breakfast."

I wanted to acknowledge that no strategy or innovation would succeed in our school district unless we addressed culture first. I had learned from previous teaching and administrative experiences that exceptional performance was only possible when there was a healthy and collaborative organizational culture. For my new colleagues in Ithaca, I noted that the "Us" versus "Them" mentality that had dominated my recent transition conversations needed to cease. Racial tensions, growing achievement gaps, and stalled contract negotiations with the teacher's union had steadily fomented a culture of low morale and negativity.

I went on to share some anecdotes, stories, and comical situations as I stressed the need to build relationships prior to engaging in the formation of continuous improvement systems and structures. I sensed the crowd relaxing a bit as I promised the culture we would cultivate together would not be *my* culture, but rather *our* culture.

CHAPTER TWO

CULTURE IS IMPORTANT

After proclaiming, "Culture Eats Strategy for Breakfast" during my first public remarks to the ICSD staff, I received dozens of emails asking for additional clarification. Those seeking more information questioned why I did not focus exclusively on the policies and systems that lead to better student success. Concerned staff expressed their dislike for the "Touchy feely stuff." They

> *A Culture of Love provides social motivation to persevere with the increasingly demanding work associated with teaching and learning in public schools.*
> *#CultureofLove*

expected me to be the hard charging leader that would force change in terms of resource allocations, curriculum, communication, and other systems perceived to need drastic improvements. Several folks went so far as to question whether I had the technical expertise to lead their large organization in New York state which has different "Rules" from my native state of Virginia...

Cultural change reaches far deeper and requires much more conversation and strategy than the policies

5

that govern an organization. In my experience, school districts are generally institutionally oppressive organizations. Oppression describes a set of practices, traditions, norms, definitions, and policies that hold down one social group to the benefit of another. In order to oppress others, a group must hold institutional power in the organization. Holding institutional power permits one group to control resources and allows it to impose its worldview. In schools, the curriculum, assessments, supplemental resources, and learning environments are examples of core programs and structures that impose one culture over the others. The norms that permeate public school culture are circulated and reinforced in schools in a way that make it very difficult to avoid believing or questioning them.

The difficulty in challenging the cultural norms in schools and other organizations is further complicated by social stratifications that position one group as more valuable than another. The historical and current relationship of inequality between some key social groups in the United States sets the stage for such a climate.

For example, white people have long been perceived to be more valuable than people of color, men more valuable than women, and the middle-class and wealthy as more valuable than the poor. The *undervalued* groups usually receive less access to an organization's resources. The perceived *more valued* groups are referred to as dominant and the perceived less valued groups are mostly referred to as minorities. Terms used to describe these relationships of inequality between dominant and minority groups typically end in "ism," like racism, classism, sexism, and ableism.

My assertion that school districts are institutionally oppressive is affirmed by student achievement data, enrollment patterns, and staffing ratios. Why are the majority of teachers white, middle-class females? Why are the top leadership positions most often held by white males? Why are young people of color and of lower socio-economic background performing worse than their white counterparts, and not gaining access to the best experiences our schools offer? School districts are institutionally racist, classist, and sexist as the individuals and social groups implicitly or explicitly target and discriminate based upon race, class, gender, and disability.

Consequently, questions from staff regarding my experience with budgeting, instruction, and New York state compliance systems did not intimidate me. Instead, staff reservations about me along with their emphasis on various systems affirmed my belief that too little time had been spent on building a positive culture. Back in my new office I'd located dozens of binders filled with previously implemented strategic plans, school improvement procedures, and other documented efforts to improve the very systems folks were still complaining about after decades of concentrated energies.

In response to questions about various aspects of my leadership, I began the ongoing process of educating people about the importance of organizational culture. High-performing organizations have established systems coupled with a professional, and positive culture. Furthermore, a comparable amount of time, energy, and focus must be devoted to both the systems and the culture.

Public educators often face complex problems where no obvious solutions exist. Educating all students in an equitable way is challenging due to the many social, economic, and political issues facing our communities today. In the absence of a positive school culture such challenges breed mediocrity, indifference, and inertia. A loving culture combats negativity while fostering effectiveness and productivity at extraordinary levels. In this constructive culture, confusion is minimized and optimism is high because of the enhanced communication amongst folks. Such collaboration contributes to the exchange of ideas and innovation. Therefore, organizations with this level of ethos attract and retain the best people; those who thrive in an environment that fosters success while focusing on collegiality. What's more, a loving culture provides leaders with the social motivation to persevere with the increasingly demanding work associated with teaching and learning in public schools.

CHAPTER THREE

RELATIONSHIPS, RELATIONSHIPS, RELATIONSHIPS

People are an organization's greatest asset. The people within that organization shape the culture. We are cultural architects. The establishment of strong and sustainable relationships is the critically important first step in a continuous improvement process. In school communities, the relationships with students, staff, parents and caregivers, and community members allow for the cultivation of a strong culture and much needed innovations.

My love for young people is on display every day

> *Loving leaders get people to do things that they could choose not to do.*
>
> *#CultureofLove*

as I strive to develop meaningful relationships with each student. Students wish to see leaders who are present, humble, and open to listening. Each year, I spend a lot of time speaking with students in one-on-one settings, small groups, and large gatherings. With every interaction, I seek to make personal connections and learn more about their experiences.

10

During my first months as superintendent, I organized a series of meetings that brought students together in affinity group conversations. I facilitated meetings with European American, African American, Asian, Latinx, Native American, lesbian, gay, bisexual and transgender, and students with disabilities. The conversations were organized to provide me with a unique understanding of the students' respective experiences in and outside of school.

As expected, I learned in which ways each group felt oppressed by the school system and other bureaucracies associated with their daily lives. Surprisingly, I also heard students indicate how they hoped for more inclusive experiences and that they themselves desired to become more inclusive of others. During these unprecedented conversations in our school district, I was able to inspire the respective groups into action. Together, we took steps that resulted in significantly more interactions and connections amongst our school district's young people.

I was once asked in a community meeting by a longtime resident, "What happened to all of the racial tensions and fights at our high school? I don't hear of any issues." I responded with, "All of those kids are now on teams together, practicing with one another,

11

competing with one another, and performing together."
More purposeful and thoughtful linking of students from
various backgrounds contributed to increased
acceptance and a more student-led culture within our
school buildings.

An example of this shift includes the
enhancement of co-curricular programs resulting in
increased diversity of athletic and academic clubs and
sports. In 2011, 43% of students in the ICSD participated
in a co-curricular program before or after school. In
2017, that number had increased to 69% of the total
population, to include a striking increase in the number
of young people of color, students living in poverty, and
students with disabilities. Along with increased diversity,
the expanded co-curricular involvement was additionally
important because of the many obvious benefits
associated with participation in athletics, clubs, and the
performing arts. Research and personal experiences
support the notion that students who are involved with
co-curricular programs exhibit the following:

- Higher G.P.A.s
- Better attendance
- More leadership abilities
- Fewer disciplinary referrals
- Higher self-esteem

- Lower drop-out rates

In addition to increased co-curricular participation, more of our young people enrolled and received support in our school district's higher-level course offerings. Too often in schools across the country, students are stratified based on perceived ability, intelligence, and achievement. This system of *tracking*, *ability grouping*, or *leveling* results in unequal educational opportunities. However, educators' and community support for differentiated instruction, academic support programs, and the removal of other barriers led to enrollment pattern shifts. Such successful efforts in the ICSD resulted in the Advanced Placement (AP) College Board recognizing our school district for increasing diversity in our AP courses, while also increasing overall achievement in those courses.

As students had more-and-more opportunities to engage in dialogue with peers from different backgrounds, it helped build necessary bonds, camaraderie, and trust. The culture in Ithaca began to shift. I established a Student Superintendent Advisory Council that includes student representatives from our middle and high schools. This diverse group of young people provide me with continuous and valuable feedback on most of the school district's strategic, innovation, and operational initiatives. This group of student-leaders has been an important partner and collaborator on code of conduct issues, mobile device initiatives, internet filtering, dress code, communication, co-curricular offerings, class size, race relations, and many other important topics. They also communicate amongst themselves and their peers on the importance of cultivating a loving school culture.

Much needed shifts in teaching and learning and other topics relevant to the student experience emerged through these interactions. Additionally, I have been comfortable sharing my thoughts and reading those of my students via social media. Empowering our youth and providing them with a voice has proven to be an essential element in achieving our

> *The statement from an educator, "You don't have to like me, but you need to respect me," is obsolete and wrong! Today, we must build strong relationships to engage, educate, and empower students. #CultureofLove*

mission. Along with student connections, cultivating strong relationships with community members is an important part of establishing a loving culture. Communicating and sharing with large groups of interested stakeholders will always be an important and necessary strategy for leaders. However, the one-on-

one and small group connections are most critical to one's culture building success. Since my arrival to the community, and as often as I can, I ask to be invited into homes for dinner, conversations over tea, family gatherings, places of worship, and any other setting for informal opportunities to learn and talk. While building relationships with families, I also gain a better understanding of the various cultures that exist within our community. In addition to spending time with individuals and families, I also utilize some formal methods in building relationships and a common mental model. Each year, I facilitate a series of visits and listening sessions with community groups and staff at a variety of non-traditional venues. These community conversations offer an opportunity for stakeholders to share their vision of success regarding our school district. Guiding questions are used to spark sharing and qualitative data are captured at each session. We also use Tele-Town Hall phone calls and other technology to engage our community in transparent two-way dialogue.

CHAPTER FOUR

A COMMUNITY OF THINKERS, THE CORNERSTONE OF TRANSFORMING ORGANIZATIONAL CULTURE

I often say that the community is the school district, and the school district is the community. In the ICSD, we believe that everyone should be involved in the education of our youth. Parents, teachers, civic leaders, board members, students, alumni, and others play an important role in influencing the educational culture in our city.

We envision the existence and engagement of all youth and adult thinkers. Accessing the intellectual power of a community's people is foundational to the development of self and society. Such thinking is the cornerstone of all creative ideas and problem solving, new scientific discoveries, new products and services, individual and organizational learning, education, business success, interpersonal and intrapersonal communications, all social change including democracy itself.

In promoting this vision, in the ICSD we share

space, time, and intellectual capital as ways of blurring the line between school and community culture. School district and community spaces are open to all for athletic events, performances, meetings, gatherings, and more. The formal and informal conversations that occur when connecting in shared spaces are transformative and trust-building.

Moreover, we encourage the sharing of time and thinking by supporting educators to become active in our community and to serve as civic leaders. Today, many ICSD educators sit on non-profit boards and engage in other local leadership roles. Furthermore, this has proven to be an exceptional way to retain staff of color while increasing diversity of thought within prominent community organizations. The educators from diverse backgrounds that were recruited to our school district have forged strong bonds with local leaders and other professionals as they serve in leadership capacities for other associations. Likewise, while ICSD educators are encouraged to serve other civic organizations, members of the local community are encouraged to actively participate in the school district's strategic, operational, and governance work.

Therefore, the ICSD Board of Education consists of a very diverse group of male and female community

17

leaders representing mixed experiences from various areas. Their commitment to embracing these differences with humility, patience, and openness has helped the governing team shape thoughtful and creative solutions to complex challenges. In other words, diversity among board members is good, but working together is what makes the board great. Individuals do not transform culture, but great teams lead sustainable change efforts.

I have the extreme good fortune, of experiencing a Culture of Love first hand where the ICSD Board of Education is concerned. This love manifests itself in that board members make it

> *Good boards make change happen, not individual board members.*
> *#CultureofLove*

possible for me to navigate my dual roles; that of school district leader and of father of two young children. They recognize that my family is among the learners served by our school district. Drawing on their unique life experiences, board members have made it clear that they expect me to be an outstanding father and community member first, then a superintendent. Each board member has provided me with friendship, mentorship, and guidance, which has allowed me to be a happy and engaged parent and an active community contributor.

Their commitment to me and my family reminds me in a tangible way, every day, of the volunteer board of education's love for young people. It has also provided me with the support and reinforcement required to flourish as a school leader. I believe that the loving relationship I share with our board of education is the seed from which our district-wide Culture of Love has grown. Without their commitment to youth our unprecedented levels of academic success would not have been possible.

Together, the ICSD Board of Education and I have established an approach to governance and leadership that recognizes student achievement is only possible when we truly open our hearts to the diversity of human experiences in our community.

We also adhere to and value a wide range of problem-solving processes. We have developed this relationship over years of small and whole group conversations that built relationships and trust. This type of working relationship between a board of education and the superintendent is essential to the success of any school district.

CHAPTER FIVE

THIS CULTURE OF LOVE, WHERE IT BEGAN...

My parents raised my siblings and I in a small rural town in Central Virginia. Our humble upbringing was rich with love. My dedicated parents were kind and patient as they supported my academic growth and social-emotional needs. My father drove an 18-wheeler for 40 years, while my mother served as a teaching assistant in an elementary classroom for 44. The amazing love my siblings and I experienced at home was coupled with a special love we received at school. My school experience included many talented educators, inclusive classrooms, emotional support, together with personalized teaching and learning strategies. My personal and professional successes would not have been possible without this combination of a loving home and an encouraging school environment.

> *Our work is much larger than graduation rates, test scores, and other achievement metrics-our work is about enhancing and saving lives.*
> *#CultureofLove*

My rich school experience included participation in outstanding co-curricular programs. I was a popular teenager in my small community as I was not only a good student, but also a three-sport athlete on very good athletic teams. Along with frequent congratulatory remarks, I was often approached by folks in the community wishing to share their thoughts on my academic future. They liked to analyze our athletic team plays, offer suggestions for potential areas of academic or athletic improvement, and more.

This barrage of constructive feedback contributed to the supportive environment needed for inspiration and accountability. Additionally, mentors and supporters did much to assist me with goal setting. Academic goals for grade point average, test scores, and attendance were combined with marks for athletic participation and performance. I enjoyed sharing news about my endeavors in the classroom and in athletic competition. At the end of a school day or game, I welcomed friends' and family's inquiries about my progress.

Strangely however, I cannot remember my father engaging me nor praising me on my academic or athletic performance. In fact, my dad would quickly change the subject whenever I attempted to share specific highlights about my feats in class or in a game. Undeniably, I struggled to understand why my father was the only person in my life that appeared to be unimpressed by my success as a student-athlete.

Many years later, I understood that he had instead focused on supporting me and holding me accountable for different goals. There were plenty of well-wishers, family, and friends in my life who focused on my athletic and academic prowess, and who would counsel me on what I would do next. As I continued to accomplish amazing things, they would assist me with the next area of emphasis and hopeful achievement.

My dad on the other hand, was concerned with an alternate set of targets for me. He was determined to concentrate on who I was becoming, not on what I was doing. I realize now that he didn't need to push me to achieve more. He knew early on that other people were around for that. For Daddy, it was never about *what* I was going to do, but rather *who* I was going to be. He'd ask me questions like, "Who do you trust?", "Did you forgive him or her?" I remember continuous input along these lines: "You need to be unselfish.", "Be nice.", "Be humble." I didn't know at the time just how valuable these lessons would prove to be. Others knew I would be a natural leader, but my father was teaching me to lead with love.

Today, whenever we gather, my siblings Robie, Della, Rovelle, and I all of whom are well-educated and gifted leaders, reflect on our good fortune. However, we would be remiss if we did not reflect on Tony, Warren, JP, Anthony, George, and other friends and family who are no longer with us. These young people who did not survive to adulthood were equally blessed with loving parents, athletic abilities, and intelligence. However, as a professional educator I have come to recognize how different their school experiences were from mine, and how their lives could have been altered had they been afforded the benefit of a truly loving school community.

Unfortunately, their educational experiences were characterized by strict policies, implicit and explicit biases, ineffective practices such as tracking, and the inappropriate use of resources. Athletic eligibility policies were based solely on standardized test scores, pull-out programs were isolating, and the curriculum and pacing guides to which they were exposed were designed to cover vast amounts of material to the detriment of thinking about information. These were the methods that destroyed what could have been healthy educational experiences.

CHAPTER SIX

THE WALKER ACADEMY INITIATIVE

While my siblings and I enjoyed the best of what public education had to offer, too many of my other family members and friends were severely harmed by common educational practices that failed to provide them with the love they needed to survive. Their stories don't include special moments of realized potential like mine, and instead, end tragically. Though school leadership requires us to work toward growth in graduation rates, test scores, and other achievement metrics, we must concurrently appreciate that our work can save or destroy lives.

With an appreciation for the intersection between a rigorous school experience and a loving culture, I knew immediately after graduating high school that I wanted to pursue a career in education. After teaching, I transitioned to various administrative roles. While working as an administrator in Virginia, I began formulating an approach to building a loving culture in schools and throughout the school district.

I served as an assistant principal at Walker Upper Elementary School in Charlottesville, Virginia. The

24

Walker school operated much like a middle school and was attended by every fifth and sixth grade student in the school district. I transitioned into the school building as part of an administrative team which included a new principal.

When crafting an entry plan for the new administrative team, the student achievement data along with the information gleaned from conversations with teachers and parents revealed that one of the biggest challenges facing the school was the plight of African American male students. More specifically, when compared to other student groups, the African American males at Walker received the most disciplinary referrals, had the worst attendance, the lowest grades, and the worst performance on standardized assessments. Along with Walker staff and parents, the superintendent of the school district and community members were equally concerned that most of the African American males were having negative social experiences in school. With a sense of urgency and pressures mounting, I was asked by the school district's leadership to craft a plan to address this systemic issue.

At this point in my career, I did not possess a dependable toolkit of successful experiences and strategies to solve complex educational issues. Instead,

I relied on my own personal experiences as a student, with hopes that the culture and tactics used with me during my formative years could be replicated in a different setting with a new generation of young people.

As a teenage student, I responded to high expectations, involvement in co-curricular experiences, and a peer and adult support network. Now was my opportunity to lead an effort to surround young men, who looked like me, with the kind of love that had contributed to my own personal academic success. We wanted to engineer an experience for African American boys at Walker Upper Elementary School that would change beliefs, behaviors, and outcomes for a cohort of young learners. Concurrently, I wanted the efforts for the target group to impact all learners and adults in the school building as well.

After approximately six months of planning, the *Walker Academy* was launched as a program focused specifically on increasing achievement for African American males in grades 5-6. This first-time effort of its kind began with a four-week summer experience held at the school. For four hours Monday-Friday during the summer, 50 young African American male students were immersed in an experience that involved team-building, public-speaking workshops, field-trips, motivational speakers, language arts, and mathematics skill development. I was joined by a small group of teachers to carefully plan an experience that was unlike typical existent summer school programs. Instead, we created an engaging suite of undertakings that generated camaraderie within a culture of high-academic and behavioral expectations.

The highlight of the summer program for these students was the field trips which included excursions to the National Great Blacks in Wax Museum in Baltimore, MD and the Smithsonian Institute in Washington, DC. For many of the young men participating in the Walker Academy, these summer field trips were their first ventures outside the city limits. Additionally, the young men's school experience had rarely, if ever, included exposure to African American history beyond Martin Luther King Jr. and Rosa Parks primarily mentioned during Black History month.

After an exciting summer launch, the 5th and 6th grade students' Walker Academy participation and associated support extended into the regular academic school year. Academy participants were expected to attend daily academic support sessions after school. Most of the students had lagging skills in reading and mathematics. We knew that remedial and enrichment

27

opportunities would be needed to close gaps between the African American male students and their counterparts at the school. I co-facilitated the after-school sessions to ensure student attendance and commitment.

I went a step further using my influence as assistant principal to promote structural shifts. Earlier that summer, I was tasked with creating schedules for the school's 600 plus students. I was given these scheduling duties because I was technologically savvy and had previous experience with information management systems. Evidently, I was also the newest and greenest administrator at the school, thus drawing the most undesirable responsibilities. Given this new scheduling responsibility, I was not yet aware of the significant influence I would have over the school's culture.

As I began to understand the instructional structure of the school and the nuances associated with scheduling, I quickly noticed the existence of various academic tracks. In this school, that operated like a traditional middle school, there were higher-level and more advanced class groupings as well as below grade-level and basic class groupings too. The higher-level and more advanced classes lacked diversity of any sort, and the students living in poverty and of color dominated the makeup of the below grade-level and basic classes.

I was unaware of the politics associated with my new school community. Naivety, coupled with my trust in the intellect of the young men with whom I had enjoyed summer learning, pushed me to make a daring and unprecedented move. I scheduled the Walker Academy cohort of African American males in the highest-level groupings in the school. Consequently, these young men, who had previously been referred to as disruptive and low achieving, were now in classes previously reserved exclusively for the highest achieving students in the city. In addition to being placed in more challenging reading, mathematics, social studies, and science groups, the young men were also placed into the school's exceptional band, orchestra, and choir classes. I was certain that learning to read music would translate into better performance in language arts class. I was also banking on many other benefits of enrollment in the arts including positive influences on self-esteem and leadership.

When the class rosters were released and revealed that African American male students were placed in advanced classes, there was push-back from teachers and parents who wished to protect the existing approach at instruction and tracking. At the time, without precedent and a successful performance outcome, the Walker Academy experiment was met with skepticism and resentment.

The questions from teachers and parents included: How could this new and young assistant principal do this? Why would the school administration set these young men up for more failure? Will the classes be dumbed down to accommodate the boys who aren't prepared to be there?

To quell the reticence and to possibly save my new job, I asked the teachers and the parents for their trust and patience as I sought to meet the needs of our most important stakeholders, the *students*. I claimed that all young people in the school would benefit from more diverse groupings of students. Additionally, I asserted that more challenging coursework for the African American males would promote more engagement and achievement instead of a return to rebellious behaviors. While hesitant, the teachers and the community placed their faith in me, the other administrators, and the students. This initiative could not fail!

The Walker Academy initiative exceeded everyone's expectations, including mine. Almost every African American male student who had attended the summer program, who had taken on more challenging classes, and had engaged in co-curricular opportunities, did very well in and outside of school. Placing the young men of the Walker Academy into higher-level classes immediately raised expectations for academic input and output. Also, while in classes with one another the camaraderie established during the summer months was strengthened, and these peers provided one another social-emotional support through both good and challenging times. Every advanced level grouping of students in the school now had multiple young men of color in its ranks. The other students, those who had not previously enjoyed an opportunity to hear diverse perspectives and experiences during classroom discussions, benefited as well.

The culture of the school that surrounded the Walker Academy participants and other students needed to be patient and dedicated. I'd be lying if I didn't say that the road was a bit rocky at times. Occasionally, some of the students exhibited rebellious behaviors. Oftentimes, the undesired behaviors occurred after students were asked to think and work differently than in prior school experiences. In response to any disruptive actions, teachers and staff were restorative. Instead of seeking to exclude the young men from the classroom community, educators worked closely with me and other administrators to find alternatives to suspension and isolation. Examples of the restorative approach included crafting reflective papers and small group problem-solving conversations with their peers.

Student achievement for participants of the Walker Academy and for the school overall increased each year. Data revealed that attendance was better, disciplinary referrals and suspensions were significantly reduced, grades had improved, and most Academy participants passed their state standardized assessments.

The young men of the Walker Academy had outstanding experiences which put them on a trajectory for future school and life success. The Culture of Love that surrounded these talented young students resulted in additional achievements in middle, high school, and college. I've followed the stories of the original 50 who participated in the Walker Academy. Almost all of that cohort graduated from high school, and most went on to college after receiving academic or athletic scholarships. I'm still connected to many of those young men as I follow their lives. Omari, Joseph, Brandon, and others are successful community leaders, fathers, and professionals.

The success associated with the transformative Walker Academy spread via newspaper articles and word of mouth. Similar programs began to spring up in the Charlottesville area and beyond. Eventually, I was joined by other committed African American male leaders to charter a local chapter of the 100 Black Men of America.

The founding principle of the 100 Black Men of Central Virginia was to increase achievement for African American male students through action steps including mentoring and academic skill development. Surrounding impressionable learners with love principles has continued to produce fruitful partnerships and success stories in the community. Over the years, the 100 Black Men of Central Virginia has positively impacted the lives of hundreds of students resulting in numerous national awards for leadership and mentoring, including the 2016 National Chapter of the Year for Mentoring and the 2013 National School Boards Association Magna Award Grand Prize Winner.

CHAPTER SEVEN

A CULTURE OF LOVE
IS NOT A LOVE FEST!

One of the best moments of my life was that of meeting President Barack Obama. In November 2014, I was invited to the White House to participate in the first National Connected Superintendents' Summit. One hundred of the nation's most innovative superintendents were at the White House to hear from the president and engage in discussions focused on preparing our schools to be future ready.

The invitation to the White House was special in and of itself, yet I was scheduled to take part in a featured panel joined by a teacher and Department of Education leader. Even more exciting was my invitation to address the entire group of educators and politicians immediately following the president's remarks. When

A Culture of Love refers to a set of practices and behaviors, not feelings and emotions. #CultureofLove

walking up to take my seat on stage, the summit organizer caught my attention and asked that I share how technology innovations contributed to remarkable student achievement shifts in the school district I was leading.

I found myself standing in front of 100 of the best school superintendents in the nation, members of the president's senior leadership team, and a worldwide audience watching a live stream of the event. As predicted, the question was posed, "Dr. Brown, please share with us the reason for the transformations and significant achievements in your school district. I froze as I remembered that I had been asked to speak specifically about technology innovations. However, I could not bring myself to talk about that at all. Instead, I responded with, "Love transforms schools, not technology!"

Successful and sustainable implementation of technology, effective new programs, and engaging initiatives are only possible when the organization's culture supports innovation and change. The culture must be honest, caring, trusting, selfless, forgiving, patient, and committed. In other words, the culture must include much love.

Personal experiences have affirmed my belief that leaders cannot mandate change; they can only influence it. I often say that the job description for superintendent can be simplified to a single sentence, "Get peo things they can choose not to do." Influencing shifts in peoples' behavior requires love. When using the word love, I am referring to a set of practices and behaviors, not feelings and emotions. The following chapters more clearly define what a Culture of Love is.

CHAPTER EIGHT

HONEST

A Culture of Love requires open, honest, and often hard conversations on a wide range of issues. Leaders who are reluctant to have difficult conversations are typically unwilling because they don't want to feel bad themselves. For many people, it is easier to avoid conflict and the awkwardness associated with a difficult discussion than to engage in an uncomfortable dialogue. I see this aversion as an act of selfishness. Leaders who fail to have hard conversations with others are choosing to ignore or even harm their customers. Therefore, a Culture of Love is rich with folks who engage in exchanges that are challenging.

These constructive discussions must be candid. Acknowledging progress, accomplishments, challenges, and failures is expected in loving cultures. Such frank dialogue can lead to disagreements, acknowledgement of one's own weaknesses, and thoughts about areas of needed growth. It takes work and commitment, but over time, stimulating discussions perpetually inspire truth in the spirit of cooperation instead of competition.

Honest dialogue needs purposeful framing in order to be non-threatening and sustainable. Establishing group norms right away creates the framing which in turn supports productive conversations. These group norms set the standards of behavior a team expects of its members. Explicitly stated, norms provide members of the group with a guide on how to interact with others and provide each other with feedback. Such working agreements contribute to positive relationships and eradicate negative energy. When there is negativity, members of the team can use the norms as a mechanism to quickly address it with each other. Additionally, parking lot conversations become rare as differing perspectives are honored and encouraged within the group setting.

Norms should be established when a team is first constituted. Then, those norms need to be revisited often to maintain focus and to provide opportunities for modification. For example, one summer prior to the opening of the academic school year, my newly formed cabinet reviewed how we should work together and settled on the following working agreements:

- Be on Time
- Be honest and expect conflict
- Get back to people within 24 hours

- Build up rather than tear down

In addition to the establishment and agreed upon norms drafted during the summer, the team revisited the working agreements prior to each subsequent gathering. Modifications to the norms were made organically during quarterly retreats as the group learned and grew together.

Purposeful and non-threatening framing of straightforward conversations is needed now more than ever as leaders locally and nationally are grappling with issues of diversity and inclusion. Truthful conduct was certainly on display in Ithaca in February 2018 as empowered high school students expressed their understanding and confidence in challenging institutional oppression and implicit bias.

Students, parents, and community members flooded a board of education meeting to challenge the high school's spring musical casting decisions. This was a complex and unprecedented conversation about the performing arts program. However, our school community was challenging one another on blind spots and behaviors, not only on casting decisions, but also regarding structural racism and safety for all students.

Engaging in public conversations regarding biased casting practices and other institutional oppression, was neither welcomed by local or national factions. Positive and negative attention came to the student activists who spoke out about their experiences with racism. The student efforts were then featured on *Fox News* and in the *New York Times*. Because of the national attention, members of various hate and extremist groups, including the Ku Klux Klan, white nationalists, and neo Nazis were alerted to the conversation being had in Ithaca. The extremists felt that a push to be more inclusive within the arts program in Ithaca would come at the expense of white students. The negative vitriol and resistance did not deter the Ithaca students however from continuing to make passionate pleas for a more welcoming and inclusive performing arts program. Their emotions and experiences needed to be heard.

It took much courage from our young people as they faced tough questions and push back from a local and national audience of peers, teachers, and others who did not identify with the same experiences nor recognize the biases being highlighted. Nevertheless, both students and adults were empowered by their organizational culture to engage in constructive dialogue about a complex problem with no obvious solution.

The student and adult leaders' truthful approach to addressing questions of inclusion in the ICSD Performing Arts Program is currently leading to more productive discussions and system revisions. Together, folks are working collaboratively to develop and implement inclusive and culturally responsive systems for choosing plays, making casting decisions, and increasing diversity within the performing arts. Speaking up and being candid isn't always easy or popular, however, a Culture of Love depends on it.

Horizontal accountability established through norms and honest dealings builds positive culture. Furthermore, the way leaders navigate personnel matters can also cultivate a loving environment. Often leaders of organizations need to provide feedback to a team member who has underperformed or not met expectations. In these conversations, leaders must be frank about the underperformance, but at the same time express how to be better and what to do next. Improvement plans, follow-up conversations, and ongoing coaching are strategies I've found effective when developing leaders who have hit and missed the mark in a Culture of Love. Handling improvement and transition conversations with dignity and support builds positive relationships and trust.

CHAPTER NINE

CARING

My mother reminds me often that people will forget what you say, but they never forget how you make them feel. We must develop an appreciation for the lasting impact we have on one another. A positive impression contributes to the development of collaborative connections. Such networks are essential in a Culture of Love. In their book, *How Full is Your Bucket*, Tom Rath and Donald Clifton assert that each of us walks around with an invisible dipper. That dipper can be used to fill other people's buckets by saying or doing things that increase their positive emotions. The dipper can also be used to dip from one another's buckets by doing things that decrease positive emotions.

> *Each person we come into contact with is dealing with something. Be nice!*
> *#CultureofLove*

Organizations fostering a Culture of Love are deliberate in inspiring folks to fill each other's buckets with compassion. Basic kindheartedness involves people sharing nice notes, positive words, recognizing achievements, and affirming efforts. Caring leaders encourage this type of culture when walking around and interacting with others. When networking, leaders must seek to find the positive in every situation and must never be too busy to inspire others. Everyone is dealing with something, so be nice!

> *People will forget about what you say, but they will never forget how you make them feel. #CultureofLove*

I've always encouraged folks to bring their kids to work. The energy that young people bring into the workplace contributes to a positive culture. When I see children of employees in the central office, I am certain to acknowledge their presence and often ask them to be sure to stop into my office during their visit to the building for a conversation, good book, or some other welcoming gift or token. This attentive gesture towards one's child does as much for the employee as it does for the young person and further contributes to a Culture of Love.

In addition to recognizing children and other family members when they visit the office, I make efforts to support team members' families outside of work as well. I seek to learn of a co-worker's connection to a co-curricular program, community organization, and events associated with one's hobbies. After gathering information, I make every effort to attend the events, games and gatherings outside of work that co-workers are connected to.

In the same way I make efforts to get to know and support co-workers outside of work, I provide opportunities for folks in the organization to get to know me as well. In an effort to extend the Culture of Love beyond work hours and the work place, I often open my home for informal gatherings and I too share information about my hobbies. A Culture of Love expands beyond the workplace. To build the relationships that sustain our culture, it is important for a team to know about one another professionally and personally.

CHAPTER TEN

TRUSTING

Trust is established when you rely on someone else. This faith can be expressed in the way feedback is elicited and how it is used in decision-making. In loving organizations, folks are provided opportunities to share their thinking and hear from others. In school districts, this two-way dialogue between students, staff, parents, and members of the community allows for perspective sharing, thinking, and problem-solving. Online feedback gathering tools, face-to-face community conversations, and clearly established communications protocols are ways of encouraging and engaging in constructive interchanges. Such purposeful inclusion of multiple perspectives builds trust in the leadership.

Trust in leadership is strengthened when the primary customer has confidence that they are the focus of all continuous improvement efforts. In my school district we have been very clear that the primary customers are the students. With students being the most important constituent, trust is built on the evidence that all processes and decisions are initiated to benefit young people. Such evidence can be seen in action and heard in the words used by leaders. For example, in addition to student-focused decisions, every day of my career I've publicly and privately needed to alert someone of an adult-centered effort or decision. When leaders center their attention on the primary customer and involve multiple perspectives in decision-making processes, the organization's culture becomes more trustworthy and unselfish.

An important, but often overlooked part of gathering feedback is one's ability to listen. Listening allows for leaders to identify the needs of others and to gather information about peoples' experiences. With this valuable information, leaders can build rapport with others and adjust organizational improvement strategies. Listening is a skill that can be developed and enhanced through workshops and practice.

I've sought opportunities to enhance my listening skills through professional development and practice. I've also allocated time and resources for my leadership teams to hone their skills as well. To improve listening skills, we encourage storytelling and pay close attention to the details and viewpoints shared by the speaker. Additionally, we focus on the questions asked by those talking. We recognize that most questions have an associated explicit and implicit meaning. We refer to this as the question behind the question. For example, those wishing to learn and collaborate use the words "How?" and "What?" often. Whereas, those looking to blame and judge use words like "Why?" and "Which?". To build trust, everyone must be mindful to listen more!

Along with encouraging and processing two-way dialogue, the leaders of loving organizations are also clear in terms of how decisions are made. Whenever possible, decision-making processes should transparently outline who has input, when, and how input will be elicited, and who will make the final decisions. Sharing specific details about the decision-making process reveals a trust in others. Involving students, teachers, and community members in strategy formation, continuous improvement efforts, and hiring practices demonstrates a leader's commitment to inclusiveness and the cultivation of trusting relationships.

> *Worry ends where trust begins.*
> *#CultureofLove*

There are some exceptional situations where excluding the community is necessary. For example, the need for confidentiality in vetting and hiring new school leaders is essential in drawing top quality candidates to apply. Nowadays, when hiring processes are public, the candidates receive intense scrutiny. Work experiences

47

and personal backgrounds are shared via newspapers, blogs, and conversations. A public vetting can result in the best candidate being chosen, however, the applicants not selected are left to navigate the complexities of the public process. The aftermath of such scrutiny can lead to an awkwardness with their current colleagues and with any others who were aware of the candidate's wishes to transition into a new role. Due to public scrutiny and the uncertainties of being chosen for an opening, many talented individuals decline invitations to participate in public search processes. Therefore, in Ithaca we've chosen to make our hiring processes confidential. It is important to note that leaders in any organization wishing to implement a confidential hiring process must first earn stakeholder confidence.

CHAPTER ELEVEN

SELFLESS

Loving leaders demonstrate selflessness through their approach to decision-making as well as in their support for colleagues. Organizations promoting a Culture of Love are explicit in how individuals will formally and informally support one another. Mentoring programs, grow-your-own initiatives, and other strategies to invest personal time into one another are an indication of unselfishness. Such continuous efforts contribute much to the retention of talented individuals and must be a priority for leaders in a loving culture. It is also important for leaders to actively seek to increase diversity in the organization. I've challenged leaders to identify an individual to support, guide, and mentor along that person's leadership path. I also advocate that those in the role of superintendent purposefully seek out underrepresented persons to mentor and support.

In addition to sharing human capital internally, loving school districts encourage students and employees to give personal and professional time for the good of others outside of the learning organization as well. Active participation in social and political causes, mentoring, and community service are cheered in the ICSD. For example, educators in Ithaca are encouraged to share their perspectives as members of other community agencies and non-profit boards. I've found that supporting educators to serve in other organizations is also a great retention tool as community service further deepens one's commitment to the community.

CHAPTER TWELVE

FORGIVING

Forgiveness is a loving action that I struggle with most. Forgiving someone is not easy as it is rare that I spend significant restoration time with a person who I perceive to have done something wrong to me. I struggle with forgiveness even though I understand that releasing anger allows me and the person in need of exoneration the opportunity to heal. Instead of healing, I have become very good at hiding my true feelings. In other words, I do not allow bitterness to impact my positive temperament, though obviously a grudge could at times cloud my perceptions and interactions with some folks.

In fact, for several years, I held bitterness against one of the best leaders I've ever worked with. This leader had openly questioned my leadership in a public meeting. The administrative leader felt that I had purposefully neglected to address an academic issue facing a specific school building. Not only did I feel that the admonishment of my leadership was unwarranted, the assertions in a public meeting with hundreds of community onlookers was inappropriate from my perspective. As a member of my administrative leadership team, how could this person speak out against me publicly? For several years, I did not mention how I felt about this situation nor how it angered me. While that same leader continued to do amazing things for young people in our school district and community, my resentment prevented me from acknowledging and appreciating their many amazing efforts.

During a reflection session focused on the love principles, each member of my administrative team was asked to reveal the loving behavior they needed to personally improve upon. As always, I was an active participant in the team meeting, and as fate would have it, I was paired with that same leader whom I had not yet forgiven. I shared that I had always struggled with forgiveness, and that frankly I was holding onto a grudge towards them. To my chagrin, the administrator shared an alternate interaction that had resulted in them holding a grudge against me as well. Our honest conversation had been long overdue. Reviewing the situations that had led to mutual grudges from one another's perspective revealed that we had both overreacted and should therefore no longer be in conflict. Through our conversation, we realized that our thinking and efforts were in fact aligned. We were then able to forgive one another, and our relationship blossomed.

In this situation, forgiveness led to a stronger relationship between colleagues. We avoided continued resentment and fear that had resulted from a lack of communication and forgiveness. When there is a lack of forgiveness in any organization, fear of disagreement and retaliation dominate the culture. This form of anxiety and lack of safety stifles improvement efforts and innovation. In a Culture of Love, folks need to feel confident that their mistakes and failures will be met with forgiveness and addressed as opportunities to grow. A forgiving culture removes the fear that one will be judged and not provided a chance to recover after a mistake. Forgiveness leads to loyalty towards the person showing compassion and to the overall organization.

CHAPTER THIRTEEN

PATIENT

People are a school district's most important resource. As with all organizations, the most important resource typically presents numerous challenges and arduous situations. When leading people in a Culture of Love, the approach must be supportive and restorative. Students, staff, parents, and community members deserve patient and humble leaders who transparently handle situations with respect and care. I feel strongly that you cannot fire your way to a Culture of Love, you must develop it! To develop people who will thrive in a loving culture, leaders must support folks who take on challenges and risks. When those folks make mistakes or fail, leaders must make every effort to restore.

Along with being understanding towards people, patience is also needed when nurturing desired results. Too often school communities seek quick turnaround efforts. These strategies may include changes in leadership, new instructional programs, and data manipulation. However, the complex problems facing school districts are not solved with quick fix tactics. A loving culture requires leaders to focus on key strategies and a commitment to seeing those things through. If long sustained positive outcomes are desired, the process for obtaining those results must be loving and embraced as much as the end results. While a lack of results must not be ignored, the way in which leaders respond to suboptimal performance is as important as the response when results are excellent.

When transitioning into my role as superintendent in Ithaca, I promised the board of education that I would lead the elimination of race, class, gender, and disability as predictors of academic success. I boasted that we could accomplish this within a few school years. Specifically, I noted to the board during my interview process that we would eliminate disproportionality in special education identification rates and the achievement results between those students with special education designations and those not identified.

After a year in my role, the board of education asked for an update on the identification and achievement data for students with disabilities. After one year, the data was worse! The data I shared with the board of education revealed that our percentage of students identified as Special Education had increased significantly above the state average. The graduation rates and test performance for students with disabilities had gotten worse.

The response from the board of education, the community, and staff to these unflattering results provided us with a sense of where we were in our establishment of a Culture of Love. I had anticipated minimal changes to data while we were in the early stages of systemic changes. Shifting mindsets, changing student and teacher schedules, professional development, and other improvement strategies needed time to take hold. However, I was worried that my new school community wouldn't have the patience to trust in their new leader. Thankfully, my fears were misplaced! Instead, when presented with the data, folks responded with learning questions, constructive feedback on the strategies used to date, and offered suggestions for additional tactics in addressing the achievement issue that had long been problematic for our school community. Instead of judging my efforts and scorning me for a lack of promised results, I was provided thoughtful support and encouragement to continue with the improvement process. Ultimately, my team and I continued implementation of the Special Education Improvement Plan developed during my first months on the job.

ICSD educators' patience with the process, along

with the restorative approach afforded me from the board of education and community, was a critical juncture in our story. Their response to the suboptimal performance was as important as what eventually became a data point we celebrate.

Two years after presenting declining data, I revealed data that showed a shockingly positive shift in identification numbers, increased graduation rates, and other achievement indicators for students with disabilities. I am convinced had the community not embraced patience, these results would never have materialized.

CHAPTER FOURTEEN

COMMITTED

Shortly after arriving in Ithaca to serve as superintendent of schools, I was interviewed by a local radio personality. While on the morning show, the host asked me the following question, "In 7-10 years, what will be an indicator of your success here in our school community?" After a long pause, I responded, "One indication of our success will be if I am still here."

The Brookings Institution (2014) suggests that the typical superintendent tenure is three to four years. An impatient community, clashes with the board of education, and the desire to move on to greener pastures are the top reasons identified for leaving. From my perspective, a lack of dedication along with the absence of academic progress in school districts also contribute to short superintendent tenure.

A Culture of Love perpetuates commitment to the organization's vision and mission for multiple years in both good and challenging times. This dedication is exhibited within all groups connected to the organization, especially the leaders.

Every day, folks in my school district are tempted by flashy new programs and initiatives that are not consistent with the school district's priorities. Our team is immune to distractions because of our commitment to clearly defined strategic efforts. Regardless of the circumstance, leaders in loving cultures stay focused on key initiatives and levers instead of abandoning plans for the next best thing. This commitment also cultivates an appreciation for the process of continuous improvement, which is equally important to the results.

As the leader I have stayed steadfast to key levers, but it has also been extremely valuable and important for folks to stay committed to me too. The board of education, students, staff, and community have recognized both my strengths and my weaknesses. The good decisions and shifts that I've made have been outnumbered by missteps and failures. Hiring the wrong person for an important role, several failed technology implementations, and a few communication missteps are examples of things that did not go well under my leadership. However, the Culture of Love that has been established in my organization is forgiving, patient, and committed.

Cultivating a Culture of Love takes many years of persistence. It is not uncommon for people to become frustrated and angry with the pace, commitment, efforts, mistakes, and people associated with establishing a loving environment. When committed to the process however, the culture becomes sustainable regardless of who enters or exits the organization.

CHAPTER FIFTEEN

MISSION IS WHAT WE DO, OVER AND OVER AGAIN, TO ACHIEVE OUR VISION

It is customary for a transition in leadership to be accompanied by an elaborate strategic planning process. The enthusiasm of new leadership, coupled with a community's desire to see changes, generally leads to a process that involves various stakeholders coming together. Then they craft intricate documents filled with goals, strategies, and data points.

However, the ICSD Board of Education and community had emphatically shared with me the extent of their *Strategic Planning Fatigue*. Prior to my arrival, the community had been through several planning processes in drafting a vision statement, mission statement, goals, and priorities. Ironically, very few people were engaged in the process and hardly anyone could recite the school district's vision, mission, or priorities.

It didn't take long for me to realize that a non-traditional approach would be required in crafting a

61

vision and plan for change. Obviously, our school district needed a clear vision and mission. However, if we had told people we were delving into more strategic planning, folks would have rebelled. Instead, I began by hosting a series of conversations to engage community members in a variety of locations throughout the district. I visited in hour-long sessions, listening to community groups and taxpayers at a series of non-traditional venues. Hair salons, barbershops, community centers, playgrounds, private homes, and places of worship were filled with excited people eager for dialogue. Everywhere we went, we asked people what they thought the district was doing well, and what it could do better. These community conversations offered an opportunity for the public to share their vision of success regarding the ICSD.

The idea behind *community conversations* began with a simple premise—our community is rich with ideas, thoughtful engagement, and strategies to move the district forward from good to excellent. While participants may have been tainted by past obstacles or mistakes, they were asked to think differently, to propose creative solutions, to suggest effective problem-solving methods, and to examine untapped resources. This tactic was necessary in breaking down the many walls created during the *us vs. them* era. By pooling good thinking surrounding growth and improvement, the community became an active participant and an agent of change in their school district.

The data captured from the community conversations was used to inform our new vision and mission. Unlike previous strategic planning processes, our new vision and mission weren't created by a small representative group, that yielded paragraphs filled with jargon and common language. Consequently, our vision and our mission statement were informed by many, they are simple, and easily remembered:

VISION: 6000+ Thinkers

MISSION: Engage. Educate. Empower.

We envision 6,000+ thinkers. This number encompasses the students and adults in our learning spaces each day along with the community of supporters who make our work possible. Our vision is what we aspire to be. It motivates us. Our vision is audacious.

Our Mission is to engage, educate, and empower. Mission is what we do over and over again to achieve vision. We

> Engage, Educate, Empower.
> #CultureofLove

strive to engage all students in the importance and relevance of thinking; to educate every learner to communicate, comprehend, and collaborate for understanding; and to empower all in the ICSD to achieve academic excellence.

I wanted every person in our community to know the school district's vision and mission. The vison and mission statement must be bold, clear, and direct. If successful, the vision and mission should be memorized by all associated with the organization. We put the vision and mission on cool t-shirts and posters that inundated the community. Folks wearing our school district t-shirt in grocery stores and at community events did much to share our vision of success. Through communication, inspiration, and relational trust, people believed in our mission, and in our ability to deliver on that mission. Thousands of community members quickly reciting and believing in our school district's vision and mission was a great start, though our overarching goal was to establish a common mental model for what the vision and mission look and feel like.

CHAPTER SIXTEEN

ENGAGE

Educators often use the word *Engagement* when expressing desired characteristics for an ideal learning environment. In my experience however, very few educators have a deep understanding of what engagement looks and feels like. Conversations and professional development opportunities with a focus on deepening our understanding of engagement were a first step in Ithaca. Using Phillip Schlechty's, *Engaging Students: The Next Level of Working on the Work* as an anchor text, we spent two years reflecting, observing, and constructing a common mental model of the level of engagement we wished to see most prevalent in learning experiences. While learning about the different levels of student engagement, educators in Ithaca were concurrently immersed in a learning experience that produced high-levels of engagement amongst themselves as well. Consequently, while learning how to engineer an engaging experience for students, educators became more and more engaged in their own learning.

Engaging professional development sessions were crafted to help teachers and administrators discern between the various levels of engagement including rebellion, retreatism, ritual compliance, strategic compliance, and true engagement.

Schlechty purports that learners who are in rebellion are completely disengaged from instruction and simultaneously involved in their own agenda and seeking their own goals. Oftentimes such students create disturbances in learning settings and encourage others to be distracted as well.

Whereas, retreatism is when learners are not participating, are cognitively disengaged from instruction, and thinking about other things. Learners who are in retreat do not consider the instruction relevant to their lives. Learners who are ritually compliant invest the least amount of cognitive effort needed to meet minimum standards and consequently have a shallow grasp of content. Strategic compliance is when the learner's goals revolve around personal goals like grades, class rank, college acceptance, and approval of others. Learners who are strategically compliant often learn at high levels, but the learning does not hold deeper meaning.

When visiting classrooms, it is possible to see students at every level of engagement, however, in Ithaca we clearly state that we want all learners to be truly engaged most of the time. Engagement is when students are learning at high levels and have a firm understanding of what they have learned. Engaged learners retain what they discover and can then transfer their acquired knowledge to new contexts. Students who find learning activities personally meaningful and challenging also persist in the face of difficulty.

Professional development must therefore include opportunities for educators to discern between true engagement and other behaviors. This revelation and learning requires much thinking, observation, and conversation. To frame discussions about true engagement, I often share videos depicting young people exhibiting these desired behaviors and high-levels of thinking. One of my favorite examples is a short film about Caine's arcade. The film features nine-year-old Caine Monroy who spent his summer vacation building an elaborate DIY cardboard arcade in his dad's used auto parts store in East Los Angeles. Caine's love for arcades steered him through a multi-month process of building an arcade that includes meticulously designed games, displays, security systems for his Fun

Pass, and hand labeled paper-lunch-bags for customers as take-home prizes.

After going months without a customer, a filmmaker passing through the neighborhood became Caine's first patron. Impressed by Caine's ingenuity, the filmmaker created a short movie highlighting the young man's work. After release of this short film documenting the cardboard arcade creation, a flash mob of customers showed up to make Caine's day. The film went viral and Caine quickly became an international sensation.

Caine's story is a feel-good example of true engagement. On display in the film is a 4th grader demonstrating the mastery of grade level standards for mathematics and language arts. Additionally, Caine reveals computational thinking along with an advanced understanding of design and engineering. While immersed in what many might refer to as *play*, Caine was constructing new knowledge and solving problems he found to be personally meaningful. When presenting *Caine's Arcade* to public educators and leaders in private businesses, I ask folks how often they've engineered opportunities for students and employees to use their imagination and play.

Caine's Arcade emphasizes that true engagement can occur during interdisciplinary experiences relevant to a learner's life. Similarly, the story of Moziah Bridges, the president and creative director of *Mo's Bows*, provides a wonderful example of a student's entrepreneurial thinking and innovative mindset. Only nine years old and unable to find anything on the market that fit his style and personality, Mo elicited the help of his grandmother in designing and making his own ties. Shortly after making his first ones, Mo started a small business in Memphis that soon became an internationally recognized brand. Mo's ties have been featured on Oprah, in many publications, and the company has a sponsorship deal with the National Basketball Association. Mo's story, like Caine's, illustrates how a young person can navigate complex concepts and content while learning new skills.

Mo and Caine are globally recognized examples of true engagement. Though inspiring, these popular accounts do not always resonate with folks working and learning in schools each day. When pressed for an example closer to home, I stress how the performing arts have long provided us with instances of true engagement in public school settings. The 2018 Ithaca High School Spring Musical is a shining case study involving students and community truly engaged in learning. In the end, more than 60 actors came together to deliver an astounding performance of *Hairspray*. The show had emerged after months of controversy surrounding the casting choices in the originally planned play, *The Hunchback of Notre Dame*. Feeling that the ICSD Performing Arts Program was not inclusive of kids of color and those living in poverty, students organized a protest and demanded immediate changes. After weeks of dialogue, a new, more welcoming, and inclusive show was selected. Auditions produced a more diverse cast and crew that immersed themselves in many hours of preparation for the show. These talented and committed youth will be remembered for their activism and perseverance in influencing the adult decision-makers. They will be legendary because of the real emotions that poured out onstage during four exceptional performances in front of large crowds. With much respect to the dozens of student performances I've witnessed throughout the years, I had never seen such a tremendous level of engagement.

CHAPTER SEVENTEEN

EDUCATE

Along with reflecting on the various levels of student engagement, the ICSD mission pushed our team of educators to reflect on what *educate* really means to our school community. To educate contemporary learners, it requires us to use new spaces and strategies. For example, the physical learning environments need to be culturally responsive and consistent with emerging brain research.

With today's more personalized learning, the traditional style of classroom is quickly becoming obsolete. The conventional design was based on architectural principles instead of learning sciences. Today's classrooms must use the interaction between physical space and pedagogical principles to encourage metacognition and better thinking.

Thus, the ICSD learning spaces shifted to incorporate writable desktops and wall space, hands-on and eyes-on learning tools, flexible seating options, technology that is responsive to learning needs, scaffolding knowledge charts, and other innovative tools not found in many traditional schools. Additionally, our classroom spaces tend not to include a teacher's desk at the front of the class. During a school visit, one teacher approached me to say, "It was amazing how my teaching changed when I removed all desks from my classroom." In contemporary learning spaces, students are encouraged to move around the classroom to promote collaboration with other students.

Active learning tools are used to support physical activity. Movement heightens student engagement and alertness, as students become active players in the learning environment. Lessons with movement are an empowering and exciting shift away from the passivity of sitting stationary at a desk for extended periods of time.

Our culturally responsive learning spaces are now inclusive as there is ample space for accessibility coupled with visuals that reflect the diversity of the learning community. Additionally, certain areas of the room are designated for meditation and reflection. These spaces are purposed to support mental health as well as provide an alternative to exclusion from the classroom community when disruptions occur. Such pedagogical shifts in our schools resulted in learning environments that are much more personalized than ever before.

Along with altering the physical space to educate students in a way that is consistent with our mission, we also shifted our curriculum design and assessment program. The newly engineered plans evolved to include much more creativity, innovation, critical thinking, and collaboration. The evolution included interdisciplinary project-based experiences that were accompanied by performance-based assessments.

CHAPTER EIGHTEEN

EMPOWER

Early in my tenure in Ithaca, I was admittedly unsure how to frame the final word of our mission statement. I didn't have clear examples or pictures that would easily resonate with folks. However, one thing I did know was that *empowering,* in a way consistent with our mission, would mean that the line between student and teacher would be blurred. When the culture is empowering, everyone is a learner. Furthermore, all learners have voice and choice in what and how they learn.

To achieve our vision for thinking we needed to cultivate meaningful and mutually beneficial collaborations between all of our organizations' thinkers. The cultural transformation that was about to happen in Ithaca would require student voice as an essential element. Too often, student voice is overlooked in education reform. Disinclination to gather valuable student perspectives on school change efforts is akin to a restaurant refusing to elicit feedback from those who dine in the establishment. Failure to listen to customers is an indication of an unhealthy organization.

The primary customers in a school district are the students. Young learners are the producers of school outcomes and therefore their involvement is fundamental to all improvement efforts. Because students' insights are often unheeded, their involvement would constitute an important reform in and of itself (Levin, 2000). Levin argues that education reform "cannot succeed and should not proceed without much more direct involvement of students in all its aspects."

In the ICSD, we began with targeted professional development, conversations, and structures intended to transition students away from being dependent on their teachers to being independent, self-motivated, and lifelong learners. Multiple mission moments are engineered every day by ICSD educators, dedicated to empowering students in all aspects of the schools' strategic, operational, and innovation efforts. One example of the emergence of more empowered students includes student-led parent-teacher conferences. Many ICSD elementary classroom teachers now provide structure and time for students to engage in quarterly conversations with their parents about their academic progress. During these student-led conversations, young

Students are a school district's primary customer. #CultureofLove

people own their learning as they share details about the thinking taking place in class, how well they are performing, how they self-assess, and areas that they are working to improve.

Empowering collaborations in school districts are made possible when students believe in their voice and adults listen. Such collaborations can be embraced by the organization's governing body. For example, student representatives from each of the high schools sit with members of the ICSD Board of Education at the bi-weekly public meetings. These student representatives are encouraged to maintain an active voice in each of the governance meetings and conversations. Questions related to resource allocation and policy are commonly presented by students who are now important contributors to both the mundane and controversial topics and conversations. Along with the students who regularly sit at the dais during board of education meetings, other students are empowered to speak with the district's governing body on a range of issues and concerns during public comment sessions and other mediums as well. Such student activism is another artifact of a culture of empowerment.

Like multi-member governing bodies, individual leaders in an organization can do much to empower student voice in systemic conversations as well. Each year, I convene some of our school district thinkers for the purpose of gaining valuable student perspectives. This group of middle and high school students known as the Student Superintendent Advisory Council meets monthly for a discussion with me and their peers on a variety of topics. It is mission critical to have student participation in continuous improvement efforts as they have unique knowledge and perspectives that can improve our approach to implementation. Also, if students are not committed to the change, the reform will not be effective (Levin, 2000).

My desire to empower students, coupled with building trusting relationships with young people, has led to new and digitally-enabled methods of enhancing student voice. Weekly, I issue the login credentials and account information for one of my social media accounts (i.e. Twitter) to a different student. I then ask the student to freely share their thoughts and experiences. Handing my social feeds over to students is intended to continue the ongoing conversations with, and feedback from, young people. It has become important for me to share with people all over the world what students have been sharing with me for years. The ICSD student perspective on the school day and their needs and wishes for the future, will inform not only our work locally, but also the national conversation about how to make our schools student-centered and more effective.

CHAPTER NINETEEN

MEASURING WHAT WE VALUE

My first district-wide leadership experience was in the Albemarle County Public Schools (ACPS), in Virginia. Initially, I served as an Executive Director of

> *If you change the way you look at things, it changes the things you look at.*
> *#CultureofLove*

School and Division Improvement and later became the Chief Information Officer (CIO). During my stint in one of the highest performing school districts in Virginia, I oversaw the school district's information management and accountability systems.

In this district-wide leadership position, with the support of visionary superintendent Pam Moran, I was able to pursue a flexible and innovative approach to accountability systems. At the time, state and national standardized assessment results dominated most accountability conversations. Year-end state tests were perceived to be a primary indication of school quality.

The ACPS's had recently completed a strategic planning process which affirmed the school district's desire to create structures that allowed for educators to know all students, make emotional connections, and find alternative ways to measure student achievement. A leading strategy for the school district was the realization of Professional Learning Communities (PLCs) in all schools. PLCs consist of teams of teachers reviewing student work and formative assessment data to identify trends, make decisions about student grouping, and determine necessary interventions. During these PLC conversations, educators were asked to combine their technical expertise with strong emotional connections to learners. Honest and trusting interactions ensured that the PLC conversations were non-threatening and focused on encouraging student and adult learning. Additionally, the PLC structures created an atmosphere of shared responsibility for every student's success.

The loving culture surrounding the ACPS's approach at capturing and reviewing student data led to constructive conversations. The artifacts of this shift became more-and-more evident as I traveled from school to school. One personalized approach at using data to understand student stories resulted in data walls upon which digital images of students were placed. These data walls were created by teachers and administrators and placed in lounges and offices. Right next to each smiling face was information such as test scores, grades, attendance, and class schedules. This data and information led to personalized grouping strategies, intervention programs, enrichment plans, and other strategies intended to meet the needs of each student in the school.

My colleagues in Albemarle County helped me understand the power of identifying the faces in relation to the stories behind the data. The emotional links to the students associated with numbers and percentages motivated me and other educators to acquire new and better pedagogical skills to meet learners' needs. We worked tirelessly to put emerging technology tools into the hands of ACPS students and we experimented with various other high-yield instructional strategies that were intended to get students to think more deeply about content.

The knowledge and skills acquired while working in ACPS informed my actions in the superintendent role in Ithaca. As a new superintendent, I had the opportunity to connect a loving approach at analyzing data in our efforts towards strategic organizational improvement. In his book *Good to Great: Why Some Companies Make the Leap and Others Don't*, Jim Collins states that great companies are more like hedgehogs; simple creatures that know, *One Big Thing* and stick to it. Mediocre companies are like foxes; crafty, cunning creatures that focus on many things yet lack consistency. Like great companies, successful school districts are dedicated to key structures and initiatives. Leaders in these districts recognize the differences between their core values which never change and operating strategies which regularly adapt to a changing world. In the ICSD, teaching and learning innovations, culturally responsive practices, and inclusion are key levers in accomplishing our mission and vision: Engage, Educate, Empower.

As part of establishing a common mental model for an organization's vision and mission, leaders must determine ways to measure what is valued by the community. In the same way that vision and mission development must be a collaborative effort with the community, determining accountability metrics should be a joint effort as well. Key indicators and metrics provide those inside and outside of the organization with information regarding the effectiveness of the mission and progress towards achieving the vision. A bold school district's vision of thinking along with its mission to engage, educate, and empower requires accountability metrics that are broader and more informative than standardized test score information.

After finalizing the organization's metrics, leaders can engage the community in transparent ways to review and use the captured data. It is important to stress that all the data will be used to learn and formulate improvement strategies. Too often, school communities use data solely to judge individuals and/or schools. To facilitate learning conversations, norms for data review sessions should stress the importance of using *How?* and *What?* Questions, instead of *Who?* and *Why?*

MEASURING "ENGAGE"

In Ithaca, to provide an indication of student engagement, we sought to gather data related to attendance rates, discipline, and co-curricular enrollment patterns. If students are engaged, they will be in school more often and attend classes more regularly. Significant positive shifts in attendance rates were realized as more-and-more young people became truly engaged. Students exhibited more authentic commitment to their work and took ownership of their own learning instead of simply coming to school to earn grades and course credit.

Another indication of engagement is the increased enrollment in co-curricular programs. Increasing the number and diversity of young people participating in a program before or after school became a school district priority. As an indicator of their commitment to the organization's vision and mission, and in the midst of major budget constraints and cuts, the ICSD Board of Education bravely enhanced sports and music programs.

Along with attendance and co-curricular enrollment, data related to student disciplinary infractions also provides a sense of engagement levels. Consequently, armed with a deeper understanding of how to increase student engagement, educators in Ithaca established better classroom communities. With more student engagement, educators' thinking shifted from how to enforce consequences to how to create caring environments that embrace restorative practices. The resulting changes in quantitative data were noteworthy as suspensions were drastically reduced. Consequently, traditional in-school suspension programs were eliminated in all middle and high schools. Those punitive tactics were replaced with reflection and support programs for young people in need of a behavioral intervention. Now, when a classroom disturbance occurs, in lieu of a disciplinary referral to an administrator, the student(s) involved in the incident are asked to write a reflective statement or engage in a problem-solving conversation with other students or adults.

MEASURING "EDUCATE"

Measuring our ability to educate contemporary learners requires an analysis of course enrollment patterns, reading scores, and graduation rates. Knowing the high-levels of engagement and thinking we wished to see in learning spaces, we quickly realized that young people needed to be enrolled in courses that require such thinking. Traditionally, the Advanced, Honors, and AP courses offered at school challenge students to think at higher-levels. Also, such advanced level course work is needed to prepare students for college and careers. Increasing the number of young people enrolled in high-level courses, increasing the diversity of enrollment, and tracking the achievement of all students enrolled, provides us with a clear indication of our school district's ability to educate. The ICSD enrollment patterns shifted dramatically as more young people enrolled in higher level courses, diversity increased, and the achievement levels in the courses increased as well. For the first time in history, the AP College Board placed the ICSD on their Honor Roll, and the designation continued for three consecutive years.

Other indicators of a school district's ability to educate while preparing students for college and careers include at or above grade level reading and graduation rates. ICSD teachers established a common assessment model with the purpose of gathering information about how well elementary students were reading. Teachers began administering a consistent, K-5 assessment of reading proficiency. This increased our ability to effectively monitor student growth and achievement in reading over time and to adjust instruction accordingly. Each year, more students were found to be reading at or above grade level. Also, the graduation rates skyrocketed from 78% to as high as 94%.

MEASURING "EMPOWER"

Data obtained from the previously mentioned initiatives and programs provide a sense of student empowerment. Additional quantitative data can be captured using a thoughtfully crafted survey. I collaborated with the ICSD Student Superintendent Advisory Council to assist me and others on our team to develop an annual assessment. Students understand the ICSD vision and mission, and now expect a school experience that is rich in collaboration and adult interaction. The survey we crafted together helps us gather data on whether students feel empowered by the structures and people serving in the school district. The annual survey administered in the ICSD contains some of the following statements:

- My teachers treat students fairly, regardless of their backgrounds or differences
- I have a very positive relationship with at least one of my teachers
- The work I do at school challenges me to think

The data gathered from the student-focused questions are shared with ICSD staff and community to spark constructive conversations.

CHAPTER TWENTY

TEACHING AND LEARNING INNOVATIONS

The ever-changing social, political, and economic challenges facing communities around the world require similarly evolving teaching and learning innovations. To successfully build knowledge and skills needed in today's workforce, an adaptive and innovative approach to instruction must exist in every learning space. These instructional methods should purposefully foster creativity and the cultivation of ideas.

Along with meeting the needs of a changing world, teaching and learning innovations must also reflect how students learn best, not in silos, but as active constructors of their own inquiry based, interdisciplinary practices, and in many ways, relevant to their own lived experiences. With a focus on real world issues and needs relevant to students'

> *Loving leaders teach people how to think, not what to think. #CultureofLove*

local communities, ICSD teachers were provided extra time to build curricular units focused on providing authentic experiences that promote engagement and content learning. These engineered experiences are referred to as case studies and project-based learning.

This new curriculum stresses student inquiry, creativity, innovation, critical thinking, and collaboration in the classroom. Science, social studies, literacy, math, and the arts are coordinated to build interdisciplinary connections and understanding. Furthermore, teachers engineer experiences that address relevant, local questions and problems.

All projects are designed to be responsive to local community needs and student lives. It may be that the origin of the work lies in concern for understanding and addressing a local environmental issue. Among the many catalysts for this work, the inquiry associated with case studies may grow from a shared experience found in a rich text or emerge from a common experience of injustice. Students' actions mirror professions such as those of scientists and historians. Students read complex and compelling anchor texts with the purpose of gathering evidence, building knowledge, then communicating their understanding. Case study work culminates in a high-quality product, for an authentic audience, putting knowledge and skills to work beyond the classroom. When students see the real-world impact of their actions and learning, they see their education as a tool of empowerment in the world.

An illustration of how teaching and learning is transformed via case studies and projects, involves learners at one of Ithaca's rural elementary schools. Each year, students at Caroline Elementary School find solutions to various challenges that arise in maintaining the school's beloved wilderness trail. The National Wildlife Federation Certified Wildlife Habitat was created by the school's students, staff, parents, and community as a space that improves the environment for birds, butterflies, frogs, and other wildlife.

Caroline Elementary students at one grade level conducted an examination of flooding on the trail and how the trail's three bridges might be redesigned to withstand the next significant flood. While receiving assistance from local contractors, students worked through the engineering process; asking questions, planning, creating, and revising their work as they designed and built model bridges using popsicle sticks. Next, students wrote scripts and storyboards to make a commercial asking for community-expert support in building bridges. After filming the commercials, students presented their work to various audiences.

As the curriculum shifted in the ICSD to be more interdisciplinary and project-based, other teaching and learning structures transformed as well. For example, the primary approach to assessment shifted from multiple-choice driven common assessments to performance-based approaches that included portfolios and other more personalized ways for students to demonstrate their acquisition of knowledge.

CHAPTER TWENTY-ONE

LEARNING DRIVES TECHNOLOGY

> *I'm looking forward to the day when being a tech-savvy superintendent sounds as odd as being a pencil-savvy superintendent. #CultureofLove*

Over the past decade many school leaders have relentlessly pushed to allocate considerable funds towards an increase in bandwidth, in improving student-to-device ratios, and in providing peripheral devices such as electronic whiteboards and 3-D printers. However, in many of these school districts, more emphasis is placed on new equipment than on creating a well-established vision, mission, and collaborative culture. These essential facets of an organization's philosophical and operational approach must dictate how educators use emerging technological tools. A common mental model towards the level of thinking and engagement expected in today's learning spaces, results in a more seamless and effective infusion of technology.

I've been blessed with opportunities to visit classrooms throughout the nation with the purpose of providing feedback on technology implementation. Too often on these visits however, I've noted how the technologies are increasing the instances of student retreatism instead of that of true engagement. The withdrawal I have observed is fueled by such activities as texting friends, shopping for gifts online, and watching movies instead of thinking and interacting with the lesson objectives. Without a common understanding of the desired teaching and learning outcomes, technology simply contributes to mediocre practices and minimal knowledge creation.

To assist with knowledge creation, great teachers have successfully engineered learning experiences with or without emerging technological tools. This has always been the case. As a former student and elementary teacher, I recognize the basic tenets of a successful lesson plan. Such plans include opportunities for learners to work independently, in collaboration with others, and the sharing of learning artifacts with an authentic audience. Traditionally, that independent work has involved the teacher, and a textbook or encyclopedia serving as the primary resource for information. The collaboration between learners often happened amongst those sitting next to each other in class or occasionally with those in an adjacent classroom space. Tri-fold poster board and student work posted to classroom walls was typically displayed before a sole audience; the teacher.

This approach to teaching and learning has obviously produced a lot of positive results and therefore, the essential elements of an effectively engineered lesson should not be altered. However, the acquisition of content, learner collaboration, and the sharing with a wider audience can be enhanced and achieved using contemporary technologies available to learners and lesson designers alike. In addition to having a personal smartphone in their pocket, many students in schools today also have access to a school district-issued mobile technology device. These web-enabled devices provide learners with access to a vast array of dynamically updated resources and have the potential to support more self-directed, self-assessment, and interdependent learning experiences. E-textbooks, game-based learning software, and other educational technology programs are examples of the vast array of tools available to learners today.

In addition to a classroom teacher, students now have access to the best researchers, thinkers and producers of content in the world. For example, along with daily interactions with their professional educators in classrooms, students can also access and practice exercises and instructional videos curated by such learning enhancement entities as Khan Academy. This free technological tool utilizes exceptional content and instructors to provide students opportunities to learn at their own pace in or outside of the classroom.

Like the technology-enabled transformation of independent exercises, opportunities to revolutionize teamwork and demonstrations exist as well. Collaboration with other thinkers in one's physical space is now easily combined with connections to learners from other schools, states, and countries. Exposure to and collaborations with various ethnic and linguistic backgrounds, particularly in segregated and homogeneous school populations, provides opportunities to develop sensitivity, understanding, and the embracing of other cultures. Digital technology tools are the portal supporting this exposure and collaboration. Thus, leading to an awakening and embracing of other cultures.

When demonstrating one's learning, a student benefits from the same vast and diverse audiences which also provide previously untapped perspectives and motivations. Using technology, learners can elicit responses and constructive feedback from peers and others on various learning artifacts and presentations.

Engaging with larger and more diverse audiences anywhere and anytime catapults motivation to new heights as students are no longer tethered to the school building or the one adult in charge of facilitating the learning.

Student learning drives the amount and type of technology usage in high performing school districts. The same is also true for adult learning. Quality teacher collaboration and professional development is evolving in reaction to new digital tools now available to educators. For example, grade level teacher team meetings at one school can be expanded to include teachers from other buildings and school districts as well. Video conferencing, instant messaging, shared digital documents, and other web-enabled communication and collaboration devices allow for significantly more voices and thinking in professional learning community (PLC) conversations. In addition to expanded PLC work, educators also have access to millions of other teachers, researchers, and experts via digital instruments. Such human resources provide invaluable assistance when educators are seeking to engineer high-quality learning experiences.

Engagements with an expanded audience are exciting, however, oftentimes the most important audience for any young learner is their caregivers. Caregiver involvement positively contributes to student achievement and to the development of school culture. Curriculum, instruction, and assessment are examples of school-related topics that require a deeper understanding by those entrusting their loved ones to an educator's care.

Traditionally, family engagement models involve newsletters, phone calls, and conferences. To engage a new generation of caregivers, the innovative use of contemporary technology is required. Traditional models of family engagement are buoyed by technology available to school communities. Nowadays, feedback on a student's educational progress is provided through social networks and electronic portfolios which enable students to show what they've learned via photos, videos, PDFs, links, and drawings.

CHAPTER TWENTY-TWO

CULTURALLY RESPONSIVE TEACHING PRACTICES

Millions of group pictures and selfies are taken every day. It is very likely that anyone reading this book has participated in this memory capturing experience within the last week. After the images are captured, folks typically pass or gather around the handheld device to review the snapshot. Within seconds, people search for themselves in the photo, so they can assess how they look, and then they often make note of who isn't in the picture. Imagine for a moment that your face rarely appears in any of the pictures, though you were present and smiling for each shot? What if, whenever you do see yourself in a photo, you find your appearance unflattering? Unfortunately, a lack of acknowledgement and positive affirmation is akin to many student experiences within today's classrooms.

Like group photo opportunities, classrooms represent a learning environment and a chance to build new knowledge. Purposeful or unintentional omission of anyone from the full photo experience is akin to what I and many other people of color faced growing up within the K-12 experience. Young people outside the dominant white middle-class culture are often not represented in the curriculum, the classroom design, the decor, nor in the pedagogy. I've observed learners' expressions at various levels of engagement when they notice implicit and explicit omission from the learning space and curriculum. Rebellious behaviors and other signals of disengagement reveal symptoms of a sick classroom ecosystem rather than that of a disabled or problematic student. Therefore, the implementation of culturally responsive practices is essential as school districts become more and more diverse.

Culturally responsive teaching practices are a key lever for the ICSD. Students deserve learning environments that are amenable to their cultural

> *We must change adult behaviors if we want student behaviors to change. #CultureofLove*

norms. To create environments that are affirming and reassuring for the entire student population, educators should engage in various personal and professional growth experiences. Targeted professional development can result in more awareness of the race and culture issues permeating our own lives and the lives of the students we teach.

With increased awareness of the varied cultural environments our students are immersed in at home, educators are then better positioned to cultivate learning partnerships, adjust instructional techniques, and empower young people while at school. Culturally responsive educators use student-relevant prompts and language, implement classroom rituals and routines, practice restorative justice, and infuse diverse images and resources. Such a thoughtful approach to meeting students' cultural needs creates intellectually and socially safe environments (Hammond, 2015).

In December 2017, the New York State Council of School Superintendent's Commission on Diversity and Inclusivity organized a special professional development event. The inaugural Diversity and Inclusivity Symposium of Thought Leaders attracted more than 100 superintendents, principals, teachers, and school board members gathered to explore research, best practices, and to create action plans. The summit focused on increasing the diversity of school leadership in New York state. As co-chair of the commission, I had the wonderful opportunity to lead the planning and facilitation of the event.

Beginning with the opening remarks, the entire two-day experience was engineered to be informal and collaborative. More distinctively, the speakers and facilitators used attention signals, response expectations, discussion strategies, and metaphors that were consistent with African American and Latino cultures. For example, attendees were asked to yell, "Amen" as if they were in a Southern Baptist church, whenever a statement or story resonated with them.

The overall feedback following the event was outstanding as many participants, largely white, noted they had never been involved in such a unique, thought-provoking learning experience. And although most enjoyed the workshop, some attendees noted how uncomfortable they felt throughout. The participants who were most uncomfortable revealed that the format and feel of the event was unlike any other professional development session they had attended. Incidentally, I've often noted that the dominant culture in most classrooms in the US is that of the Caucasian middle-class, and therefore typically, their professional development takes on the same look and feel. Rarely are educators put into learning situations inconsistent with their own cultural norms. However, every day most of our nation's public-school students walk into classrooms that are unlike their home environments. While the Diversity and Inclusivity Symposium of

Thought Leaders was awkward for some participants, the culturally responsive pedagogy was positively impactful for others. Specifically, attendees from diverse backgrounds experienced high-levels of engagement, education, and empowerment.

Like the experience for those attending the Diversity and Inclusivity Symposium of Thought Leaders, similar culturally-responsive experiences must be engineered for young learners in our schools. To be culturally responsive, educators must provide all students opportunities to bring their cultural backgrounds into the classroom. The curriculum is defined by *what* is taught, and *how* it is taught. Culturally responsive curriculum reflects diverse perspectives and language and provides inclusive, accurate portrayals of historical events and cultural groups. Native American, Black, Hispanic, and Asian students make up the majority of the public-school students in New York state and most other states in America. However, I often hear from the students and families in these membership groups how their school resources are laden with racist depictions, historically inaccurate facts, and biases against their culture. Culturally responsive educators pay special attention to *what* is being taught as it has a profound impact on *how* students learn.

When resources and materials represent a wide variety of cultures, then educators are equipped with needed tools to adjust instructional strategies. This allows for different learning styles that often vary based on one's lived socio-cultural realities. For example, when not in school, my children Aiden and Landyn are immersed in a collaborative environment dominated by people working together to create, analyze, and arrive at solutions. In our family, our culture supports an interdependent approach at learning. We typically work together and won't allow anyone in the group to lag behind or fail. This approach is common in African American and Hispanic homes. However, the instructional strategies that work best for my two children, which include many opportunities for small group collaborations and discussions, may not work for other students in the same classroom. Educators seeking to meet the needs of my children will need to use different instructional strategies than those used with students whose culture supports a more individualistic and competitive approach to learning, traditionally found in European and European American cultures.

Unfortunately, due to the *what* and *how* embedded in traditional curriculum, the realities for many young people in public schools include significant amounts of racism. In Ithaca we are actively working to enhance and develop curricular experiences that are not only culturally responsive, but the curriculum is being developed to also ensure that our thinkers are anti-racist. I feel strongly that the development of anti-racist understandings and practices must be accompanied with a broader grasp of anti-marginalization. The ICSD anti-marginalization curriculum will be used with every student in our school district. These curricular units (case studies and projects) are to be developmentally appropriate and touch on multiple forms of oppression, towards gender, socioeconomic status, disability, and race. The *how* associated with our anti-marginalization curriculum begins in learning spaces with all students engaged in critical thinking, differentiated instruction, cooperative learning, and collaborative grouping.

Along with ensuring the curriculum is culturally responsive, the physical environments in schools must speak to ethnic, cultural, linguistic, and learning backgrounds as well. In Ithaca, we've invested time and resources into professional development that involves educators developing a deeper understanding and awareness of culturally responsive physical environments. Administrators and teachers routinely visit classrooms throughout the school district examining how media materials, visuals, room arrangements, and technology promote inclusion and diversity while fostering student independence. After visiting classrooms, administrators and teachers engage in reflective conversations.

Learning spaces need to promote safe and affirming communities. These environments should keep relevant and current learning visible and accessible, serve as a reminder of prior learning, and enable students to make connections to new learning. With an awareness and promotion of culturally responsive learning spaces, we are then in a better position to cultivate learning partnerships and empower young people. Please take time to look at the learning environments in your organization and reflect on these questions:

- What values do you wish to communicate through the learning environment?
- How do you want learners to experience their time in the learning space?
- What do the artifacts on the walls communicate to students, parents, and others about what is important?
- What do you want the environment to *teach* those who are in it?

CHAPTER TWENTY-THREE

INCLUSION

One morning in the spring of 2014, my then three-year-old son, Aiden, made a simple request: "Daddy, may I watch some TV before school?" I figured I would enjoy of few relaxing moments with him on the couch as we snuggled to watch *Paw Patrol* or some other animated adventure. Surprisingly, while flipping through the channels, it was CNN that caught my son's attention. He stopped on a story featuring then President Barack Obama. I do not recall the topic of the feature story, and I remember that the content itself did not capture my son's attention either. What engaged my son Aiden was the image of a light-skinned African American male wearing a suit and being referred to as the most powerful leader in the world. At the same time, I found myself glancing over at the coffee table to see the mayor of Ithaca featured on the cover of the local newspaper. Like Barack Obama, Svante Myrick is also an African American male.

Unlike anything I had experienced growing up, I suddenly realized that my son was surrounded by images of amazing African American male leaders.

When I was a child, I could only dream of what it would feel like to refer to a black man as president, or mayor, and I certainly had never thought about the reality of a black superintendent of schools.

Today, my son's environment includes many public examples of black male achievement. Unfortunately, prominent examples of African American achievement are still outnumbered by instances of exclusion, segregation, and oppression. My own children still witness occurrences of such each day in their community.

My children's current reality represents change that spans several generations. Particularly, they benefit from shifts in educational experiences and opportunities. My father and his generation of peers fought for the right to go to integrated schools. My dad went to an all-black one-room schoolhouse in Central Virginia. He continued to experience school segregation as he was forced to attend an all-black high school.

Unlike my father, by the time my older brother and sister went to school, school segregation was no longer part of their experience. At that time, in the 1970's, attending integrated public school was thought of as considerable progress. While racially integrated, the classes and programs within the schools were nonetheless often, and purposefully, divided by race and socioeconomic status.

I attended the same schools as my older siblings but by the time I arrived at our local high school, educators and policy makers wished to decrease the tracking and segregation within the school environment. I was the first African American male to enroll in an Advanced Placement (AP) course at my high school. In addition to the AP course, I was taking Honors level courses. I was the only male student of color in my upper level classes. My twin brother and my friends, who looked like me, remained in *basic* or *remedial* courses. In a sense, I was *included* in high-level course offerings.

Today, my children attend a public school like my father had, in an integrated school with their white counterparts like my older siblings did, and will eventually enroll in high-level courses like their dad (me). However, unlike my experiences, the expectations for my children will be different than those of the generations of Brown family children before them.

My children's public-school experience is projected to be successful and inclusive. My children are not pilot projects, nor a token selection. My children and the educators connected to them will be held accountable for high-levels of achievement in their advanced-level studies within a very diverse school district.

The story of my family represents significant shifts toward more inclusive school opportunities. However, in Ithaca and many other school districts today, many more inclusion efforts are needed. Inclusive school communities empower learners and respect the diversity of all students. Respect for learners contributes to the high expectations for achievement and the support of multiple educational opportunities.

Traditionally, schools have struggled to create educational experiences inclusive of students with special needs, young people of color, and/or students living in poverty. Moreover, the most engaging and challenging school experiences have been reserved for students

In lieu of suspension and isolation, loving learning communities heal one another and work together seeking to understand the source of distress. #CultureofLove

perceived to be high achieving and for those who are part of the dominant white middle-class culture. Inclusion is the belief that all children belong regardless of their ethnicity, socio-economic status, need, or ability. When diversifying the classroom environment, achievement for all students increases. The incorporation of diverse thinking, backgrounds, and perspectives contribute to a culture of innovation and love.

In the ICSD, we used our professional development and curriculum building workshops to stress the reflection and action steps needed to be more inclusive. Teachers and administrators reviewed and researched various texts and other resources affirming that all students achieve better when classrooms are inclusive. We also reached a common agreement that the best approach to inclusion is to get every student to think every day.

Moving away from pull-out programs and segregated classes required patience and trust from educators. Also, teachers needed to work diligently at making needed adjustments to their pedagogy. Along with self-reflection regarding individual and collective beliefs, we developed action plans focused on making the structural and procedural shifts necessary in fostering inclusion. These shifts included additional administrative support and leadership, an improved co-teaching model, additional time for collaborations amongst teachers, flexible classroom spaces that did not isolate learners, and more differentiated instruction.

Inclusive efforts will be met with resistance. I've learned that the most difficult challenge is the mindset of educators and caregivers. My first stint as principal was at Ratcliffe Elementary School in Henrico, Virginia. Over 450 students were educated in this urban environment just a few miles from downtown Richmond. Over 90% of the students were African American and more than 90% of the school population received free or reduced-price meals. Ratcliffe Elementary did not have Virginia State accreditation due to low student achievement. In addition to low test scores, the school had a reputation for outrageous student behavior.

I knew that a culture shift would be needed at my new school to increase student achievement and regain accreditation. When I arrived, the team of educators at Ratcliffe operated several self-contained classrooms. Students with and without identified emotional and learning disabilities were segregated from their peers all day as they received instruction from a special education teacher and a teaching assistant. Even in these self-contained settings, the students often got into altercations with one another and exhibited explosive behaviors towards the adults in the room. In addition to negative behavioral expressions, low grades and test scores plagued the students, plus they rarely had any opportunity to spend time learning with peers and adults in general educational settings.

One of my first moves as principal was to disband self-contained classrooms and integrate all students with disabilities and those exhibiting severe disruptive behaviors into regular classroom settings. I also asked the special education teachers to co-plan and co-teach with general education teachers to meet the Individual Education Plan (IEP) requirements for the students with disabilities. This inclusive approach did not yield positive dividends right away. Initially, many of the adults struggled to differentiate instruction for students with disabilities and for those with significant academic skill gaps. The range of school achievement was large and the gaps in knowledge made it very difficult for educators to differentiate lessons to meet the wide range of student needs in one classroom. Furthermore, as the students with disabilities and behavioral issues were asked to complete more rigorous assignments, their responses were oftentimes disruptive. I was called to classrooms frequently in the first few months for a student who had flipped a desk or thrown an object in defiance of a teacher or peer.

I soon started receiving complaints from teachers and parents about what they perceived to be a failed experiment. Admittedly, the professional development needed for educators to effectively co-teach, differentiate, and manage the student mental health issues had not yet been provided. The professional development had begun, but we had not waited for all workshops to be completed prior to beginning the inclusion initiative. I used the analogy, that we were building the plane in the air. Along with teacher reticence, many parents were mortified that their children were exposed to extremely negative behaviors and a wide range of academic needs during regular class time.

Several staff, parent, and other meetings were requested by folks who wanted to confront the principal (me) about the inclusion initiative. They expressed their wishes to revert to the previous approach of grouping students in the school. Many parents indicated they believed that the rising crime rates in the local community were due in large part to young adults who had dropped out of high school and turned to drug and alcohol abuse. The parents felt that the behaviors some adults exhibited in the community were manifestations of the school district's inability to address such behaviors as early as elementary school. These disgruntled parents predicted that placing the most disruptive students in classes with other students would only increase the likelihood for all children to display inappropriate behavior.

I took this opportunity to remind parents that the children attending the public schools were simply a representation of their area of the city. Everyone wanted a safe, collaborative, and productive community. However, when a culture supports the exclusion of some students from the general classroom, that very mentality is divisive and destructive to all in the community. First, the alienation and low expectations expressed to the learners targeted for exclusion contribute to frustration and negative emotions. The lack of safety and support felt by the excluded students make it nearly impossible for them to learn. Years of segregated school experiences and the associated lack of school achievement contribute to many social issues that impact the overall community such as poverty, health problems, and crime.

In the absence of an inclusive culture, students who are not welcomed into the general education environment suffer due to low expectations for achievement and the lack of access to opportunities afforded other students. All learners are negatively impacted when some of their peers are omitted from the regular classroom setting. When peers see one another removed for breaking rules, exhibiting undesirable behavior, or a perceived lack of ability, the message is that one's place in that particular community is contingent on their assimilation to the dominant culture. Should we be sending that message to thinkers as early as elementary school?

Suspension, self-containment, and other tactics to remove students from a classroom or school should be rare. In lieu of exclusion, loving learning communities heal one another and work together seeking to understand the source of distress that has led to oppositional conduct and subpar academic achievement. Regardless of the situation, a Culture of Love supports meeting human needs and addresses the dilemmas that arise.

A common mindset and commitment to loving all students is the first step in becoming a more inclusive school. This shared mental model is necessary for facing the complex and ongoing challenges that will occur. With a consistent and mutual pledge to all students, leaders can then adjust the instructional and mental health structures to meet various academic and mental health needs that exist in classrooms. At Ratcliffe elementary, we focused professional development efforts on developing quality co-teaching teams and on instructional strategies intended to meet various student needs within a single classroom.

Additionally, we elicited community resources to better understand and address the trauma many of our students had experienced.

After two years of cultivating a Culture of Love at Ratcliffe elementary, the school regained accreditation. Also, the school's local and state assessment results moved from the lowest to among the highest when compared to the school district's other forty-four elementary schools. The adults had cultivated a culture that was patient, forgiving, and committed to all students. Most importantly, the culture that developed while I was there was sustainable. Many of the loving initiatives that began when I arrived have carried on regardless of my and other principal departures.

CHAPTER TWENTY-FOUR

SELF-REFLECTION

One cannot understand nor influence others until they have a deep understanding of self. Leaders in a Culture of Love must have a significant amount of self-awareness, only achieved through examining one's own beliefs, values, perceptions, and actions. Self-reflection is an important first step in operationalizing a Culture of Love as it must happen prior to any substantial changes in behavior.

The self-reflection needed to impact behavioral changes must be modeled by leaders. Members of an organization will not feel comfortable reflecting and

> *Failure is the most important thing a leader can do because it shows he/she is a learner.*
> *#CultureofLove*

taking risks unless the leaders are willing to take chances themselves, share the things they are doing, and attempt to make self-improvements. I have been purposeful and transparent with professional vulnerabilities. I've also been forthcoming with my personal improvement struggles. For example, each year at the opening convocation for our school district, I speak publicly about the areas I have identified as needing more attention in my professional and personal growth. Additionally, I share specific action steps focused on addressing the identified deficits.

Self-reflection on the loving actions described in this book is essential in developing a pervasive Culture of Love. Folks must think about what behaviors come naturally, and which actions are uncomfortable and require additional effort. As part of my personal self-reflection and modeling, throughout the year, I note the behaviors that I am spending additional time self-reflecting on with hopes that I will change my conduct.

Along with my own personal deliberations, I spark self-reflection in other leaders in the organization as well. Typically, school administrators struggle to find opportunities to reflect. Furthermore, a lack of reflection can stifle the effectiveness of gatherings intended to promote professional development.

The intensity and distractions of a typical day for administrators creates great need for self-reflection prior to any meeting or learning experience. On the way to a meeting or workshop, it is typical for an administrator to field calls from parents and converse with several staff members seeking assistance with an issue. With emails continuing to flood one's inbox, understandably, much is happening to distract or hamper an administrator's ability to fully transition to a professional growth opportunity.

Therefore, at the beginning of my meetings and presentations, I always ask folks to take a moment to reflect. This reflection protocol may include individual meditation, a short writing task, or other forms of mindfulness. Initially, there was some reticence from various leaders, as mindfulness activities are rare in professional settings. Questions like, "How does this relate to what we are doing?" and "Can this be an optional part at the end of the meeting instead?" were posed. However, there was also an appreciation from other leaders for the purposeful approach to asking very busy people to meditate and focus on self. Soon, the opening self-reflections were perceived by all to be a great way of transitioning to personal and professional learning.

CHAPTER TWENTY-FIVE

CONSTRUCTIVE USE OF CONFLICT

The behavioral shifts that occur after self-reflection usually spark some conflict and uncomfortable dialogue. Successful leaders see conflict as natural and realize that it must be used in constructive ways. When had in the spirit of cooperation instead of competition, uncomfortable conversations can shape an organization's overall culture.

As cultural architects, leaders must articulate the value and need for conflict, and facilitate open and honest dialogue to bring alignment to their cultural aspirations. While seeking opportunities to spark needed conversations, leaders must not avoid conflict. If leaders evade conflict, they give everyone in the organization a pass to do the same. If leaders are defensive, others in the organization will shy away

> *Debates rarely (if ever) change hearts. Love changes hearts. If you want to see change, love people, don't argue with them. #CultureofLove*

from acknowledging their own weaknesses, blind spots, and incompetence. While modeling a constructive approach in conflict management and in having uncomfortable conversations, leaders must also acknowledge, reinforce, and support others who engage in constructive conflict as well.

When conflict and uncomfortable conversations become more-and-more welcomed in an organization, innovations happen more often as well. If everyone in the room has the same idea, it is probably a BAD idea! Artificial consensus building never leads to true innovation. In a Culture of Love, folks challenge one another's thinking in conversations, meetings, and other interactions. When an organization establishes a Culture of Love, talented and committed people trust one another. When this trust is coupled with forgiveness, constructive conflict is embraced. The uncomfortable dialogue becomes an expression of love for a peer or colleague. Then, the conversations between contemporaries contribute to new thinking, solutions to problems, and innovations. For example, when having strategic conversations with members of my leadership team, I often take an opposing position even if I agree with an approach. Teammates tend to become a bit frustrated as they are constantly defending and evolving their position to address the concerns being raised. Ultimately, the proposition is strengthening and/or a new and better method is created.

Even when forging towards new and unprecedented levels of success, loving cultures need daily nurturing. Every day there are dozens of situations that serve as litmus tests for the strength of the organization's culture. I still witness, or someone shares with me, a specific incident that is inconsistent with the type of culture we aspire to. When these situations are brought to my attention, I do not make excuses and I am never deflated. On the contrary, when occurrences bring into question the principles of our loving culture, I use these opportunities to further embed the desired culture into the fabric of our organization. Frankly, I yearn for daily disruptions in culture as they allow for cultural fortification.

On several occasions, the leadership of one of our organization's collective bargaining units informed me of a practice by a member of my cabinet that impacted their trust. Instead of allowing the conversation to end with the reporting of a complaint, I requested a meeting with all parties. I framed the meeting as an opportunity to strengthen our culture, build more trust, and practice humility. The resulting conversations strengthened relationships and ultimately reinforced our Culture of Love. When approaching tough conversations and situations with love, rebuilding trust won't take years, instead the trust is stronger the very next day!

CHAPTER TWENTY-SIX

POLICY CAN BE OPPRESSIVE

Because policy shifts impact the culture of a school district, revisions to guiding regulations must include the engagement of the community, students, teachers, parents, community leaders, content experts, and others. The community must be invited to share their thoughts and provide constructive feedback as part of a transparent and inclusive policy development process. This process may include opportunities for public comment, community conversations, and work sessions focused on information dissemination and policy development.

In the ICSD, we started a policy revision process with the primary purpose of eliminating oppression, increasing student achievement, and cultivating our Culture of Love. We also wanted to ensure that language used in describing policies adequately reflects our current culture. Therefore, since 2010, the school district has been engaged in a

> *When looking at policy from a loving, culturally responsive, and inclusive perspective, the oppressive words jump off the page. #CultureofLove*

comprehensive and systematic updating of all district policies aimed at transforming the district's culture. The ICSD Board of Education launched a student-centered process intended to ensure that every single policy promotes – and does not impede – an environment for students and staff characterized by inclusiveness; cultural responsiveness; and loving respect.

School policy revisions can trigger candid discussions and debates. Typically, the most deliberated policy shifts occur when there is a national hot topic or emerging trend that sparks conversations about school policy. Instead of reacting to a contemporary issue or conversation, the ICSD Board of Education initiated a comprehensive policy review that sought to examine every policy with the goal of eradicating institutional oppression in the school district. No policy was considered mundane or more important than any other as each one was viewed as an opportunity to scrutinize language used to protect or remove oppressions and barriers to student achievement. Examples of the ICSD policy shifts include:

MEAL CHARGE POLICY

The policy review process led to the removal of language that referred to a specific amount owed by students along with the consequences for reaching those balances. The new policy verbiage is more forgiving and prevents lunch shaming. Previously, parents and students were notified when accounts fell below $5. Along with the notification of low balances, families felt shamed by the constant reminders per district policy and the threats to collect prior to the end of the school year to avoid consequences.

Previous language:

"...parents and caregivers shall be discretely notified of student account balances regularly. When a student's account balance falls to $5, the District will discretely notify the parent/caregiver of the balance by a nightly automated telephone call until deposit is made and posted to the student's account. Parents and caregivers will also be notified regarding this policy and the process for refilling the account. These notifications will continue regularly until the account is replenished. Parents and caregivers must repay all unpaid charges remaining at the end of the year or before their child leaves the district, whichever occurs first."

Changed to:

1. *Parents and caregivers should maintain funds in accounts to minimize the possibility that a child may be without meal money on any given day.*
2. *Allow only regular reimbursable meals to be*

charged, excluding extras, a la carte items, and snacks.

3. *Permit students to charge for a meal; provided however that parents and caregivers remain financially responsible for any meals that are charged.*

4. *Use a computer-generated point of sale system, which identifies and records all meals as well as collects repayments. Charged meals must be counted and claimed for reimbursement on the day that the student charged (received) the meal, not the day the charge is paid back.*

DOMESTIC FIELD TRIPS

Some policies needed additional language to represent a shift to a more inclusive approach to teaching and learning. For example, the ICSD school community values opportunities for student exposure to a variety of cultures and enrichments through field experiences and field trips. The culture also now supports efforts to make field trips accessible to all students regardless of finances, disability, or any other previously limiting factor. To represent this more inclusive approach, the domestic and international field trip policies were revised to incorporate new language not previously included.

The ICSD shall afford students with disabilities an equal opportunity to participate in field trips to the maximum extent appropriate to the needs of the student. Where related aids or services are necessary for a student to participate in a field trip, the ICSD shall provide those necessary aids or services. Determinations regarding whether a student with a disability can reasonably participate in a field trip, and what, if any, related aids or services are necessary for such a student to participate, must be made on an individual basis.

SPECIAL EDUCATION POLICIES

For some policies, the ICSD Board of Education elected to elaborate on language to affirm the school district's culture. When possible, language was added to stress inclusion and restorative practices.

Previous language:

The board of education shall make available to all students who reside within the District and who are eligible under the Individuals with Disabilities Education Act (IDEA) and Article 89 of the Education Law a free appropriate public education in the least restrictive environment appropriate to meet their individual needs.

Changed to:

Ithaca City School District acknowledges and values

diverse learners across our student population. We believe that all students arrive to school with skills and challenges that we must be responsive to in order to optimize the learning experience for all children. Students that are classified within the special education program are general education students first and foremost, and our district's ability to respond to the unique needs of individual students and to fully include them in this educational program are key measures of our effectiveness as a teaching and learning organization.

CHAPTER TWENTY-SEVEN

BUILDING THE LOVING TEAM

Recruiting and retaining principals is the most important aspect of a school superintendent's job. My experiences reveal that a building's principal is a primary contributor to student achievement (or lack thereof) and the overall school success. Due to the significant importance of the

> *Hire people based on their eagerness to learn, not their resumes.*
> *#CultureofLove*

school's principal, the selection process for a new leader always generates much attention from students, parents, and others in the community.

Prior to my arrival in Ithaca, the search for a superintendent or principal was an open process that included public interviews and other vetting involving multiple stakeholders. While the process had resulted in hiring me and other quality candidates, the lack of confidentiality in said process began to deter good candidates from applying for positions in Ithaca. Instead, those individuals opted for more confidential search processes in other school districts. We recognized that we needed a new and more confidential leadership hiring practice though this shift would mean excluding community members who had previously enjoyed a significant role in the open search process.

In keeping with one of the basic Culture of Love behaviors, and after much reflection and planning, I outlined a new principal selection process that requires *trust* from all involved. Whenever an opening for a new building leader becomes available, I first conduct meetings with various school and community stakeholders. In that initial meeting, I clearly outline the methods we will use for providing feedback, the process for selection, where in the process community members will become involved, and who would make the final decision. I reiterate that all activities related to principal selection are confidential. The screening, and final round of interviews are only conducted by me along with several members of my Cabinet. Again, I ask for the school community's trust in the need for confidentiality during and after the entire process as it is the best way to ensure that quality candidates apply.

While recruitment and retention of administrators is one of the most important aspects of my job, as superintendent, I must be unselfish with this very important hiring process. While filling building principal openings and any other administrative vacancy, I am transparent with my true intention, which is to hire a future superintendent. When recruiting, I am looking for leaders with loving dispositions that exude selflessness. Leaders in a Culture of Love commit to serving the organization in whatever role necessary. I believe that leadership teams must evolve to meet the needs of the organization instead of organizations changing to meet the demands of individuals.

Some of the most difficult and uncomfortable conversations I've had occurred with administrators I wanted to transition to a different role. During my tenure in Ithaca, my administrative team underwent more than 250 changes. This included talented individuals coming into the organization, leaders moving to new roles within the organization, and in some cases, leaders leaving the organization.

While it can be challenging to converse about role shifts, a leader's willingness to engage in uncomfortable conversations is also an indication of unselfish behavior and culture. It is easier to avoid tough interactions instead of engaging in dialogue intended to share information or address conflict. Though it may be easier to elude a much-needed interface, it is never good in a loving organization. Unselfish leaders delve into those difficult conversations that might easily have been avoided.

It is difficult to move folks into new roles when an incumbent leader is not seeking a professional change. For example, only one leader can serve in the role of superintendent of schools in a school district. However, I've been blessed to work with many very talented and accomplished administrators who ought not wait for me to leave prior to transitioning into the role of superintendent somewhere else. In Ithaca, administrators' expertise and experiences have contributed to many achievements for the organization and for me. Nonetheless, the selfless spirit in the ICSD supports these leaders taking on more responsibility and influence in roles that would benefit the rest of the state and industry.

At times, when talented and accomplished leaders preferred to stay in their current role, I have strongly encouraged, and in some instances *forced* them, to look for opportunities at becoming superintendent in other districts. Today, many former members of the ICSD team are currently serving as superintendent and in other key leadership roles in other school districts. Leading in a Culture of Love requires one to make unselfish sacrifices so that other organizations may be impacted by positive thinking as well.

Recruitment, retention, and development of both administrators and teachers is an essential part of the development of school culture. Taxpayers invest millions of dollars into all teachers and administrators when calculating salary, benefits, professional development, and other costs associated with the onboarding and development of a professional who spends a career with the organization. Therefore, the mission critical hiring process requires attentiveness and care from leaders of the school district.

The hiring process must include consistent ways for decision-makers to ascertain the true desires of a candidate. Potential hires must first demonstrate they are educators coming into a Culture of Love and must be able to articulate their desire to cultivate strong relationships with students and adults alike. When recruiting educators, I begin each interview with a simple request of the candidate: "Tell me how you have demonstrated your love for students." I've asked teaching and administrative candidates this question at the beginning of hundreds of interviews. The answers given in response to that first question have provided much insight into the educator requesting to join our team.

Typically, an interviewee can provide examples and experiences that reveal their disposition and hopes of engaging, educating, and empowering learners. While listening, I am hoping for expressions of one's efforts at working with diverse populations, differentiating to meet the needs of learners who struggle to achieve, and their willingness to meet the needs of young people who achieve at exceptionally high levels. I've learned over the years, that the best candidates can also share specific examples of how they validate and affirm the various ethnic, cultural, and linguistic backgrounds that exist in classrooms. In Ithaca, in order for us to gain additional insight into a candidate's experiences and aspirations, those applying must include writing samples expressing their thinking in response to the following questions:

- ICSD has a diverse student population representing a variety of races, gender identities, learning needs, social economic status, sexual orientation, languages, national origins, etc. Describe your teaching strategies and/or experiences for effectively educating students from diverse backgrounds.

- Please give specific examples of how you respond effectively to students who have a variety of identities, and/or respond effectively to students who are different from your own identity. How do you ensure success for every student?
- Tell us about any personal and professional experiences you have had that would help you help us to fulfill our district equity goals.

Finding and developing people is a priority in high performing school districts. At the same time, the staff should represent diverse backgrounds. My first day visiting classrooms in Ithaca in January of 2011 was special for many reasons, particularly because I was blessed with an opportunity to shake hands with my new colleagues. More importantly, I was privileged to meet and embrace many of the amazing young learners in my new school district.

One student introduction was one of the most memorable of my career. Shortly after walking into a 1st grade classroom, I felt a little person giving me a hug on my right leg. When I looked down I saw a bright-eyed, beautiful young African American girl. She looked up at me with those big brown eyes and said, "Hello, did you come to see me?" I responded, "Of course sweetheart, I am here to see you and every other thinker in this class." I went on to explain to all the first graders what a "superintendent" was, and how I'd be coming around often to see them. None of the children in the class knew what the superintendent does, but I quickly got the sense they all felt this new person in their space was different.

When walking towards the door to leave the classroom that day, the special education teacher co-teaching in the space tapped me on the shoulder. I was surprised to see that she was in tears, and I inquired as to what had gotten her so emotional. She explained that she was moved because of the young first-grade girl who spoke to me and hugged my leg. Apparently, the child had not spoken to any adult in the building since August. Prior to my arrival in the classroom that day, the young student had not felt comfortable speaking with other adults and yet there she was hugging my leg.

It occurred to me that this young student had reached out to someone she felt comfortable with, she wanted to connect with, and who evoked familiarity with her home environment. The student-teacher relationship is the cornerstone for thinking and achievement in the classroom. Many research studies reveal that students are more likely to develop relationships and perform better academically when they have experiences with highly skilled, well trained, and diverse educators. On that January day, I didn't need to review the mounds of research supporting the need for students to interact with an educator of color. Instead, a six-year old provided me with all the affirmation I needed.

CHAPTER TWENTY-EIGHT

WHY SCHOOL?

Most of my family members reside in and around Central Virginia. Early morning on August 9, 2017, I was conversing with my mother and father, while unbeknownst to me, white nationalists had gathered in Charlottesville, Virginia to protest the removal of confederate statues. The protest turned violent and ultimately resulted in the loss of life and an infamous moment in our nation's history.

Filled with emotion, my father shared with me a copy of his local newspaper, *The Daily Progress*. The front page revealed an image of white nationalists holding up torches while chanting racist, and anti-Semitic statements. After handing me the newspaper, my father asked, "Why School?".

Typically, this question would be an easy one for any professional educator to answer. For a successful educator boasting state and national recognition, the answer to my father's question should have flowed easily and emphatically. However, on that day, I had no answer. Later, I had conversations with family members who explained they had spoken with some self-proclaimed white nationalists as they descended upon Charlottesville.

> *Academic achievement means nothing if our graduates are not inspired to be better, more loving people. #CultureofLove*

This is how my father had learned that the protesters were largely high school and college graduates, former athletes, business owners, and people who had experienced some success in school. His question, "Why School?" was coming from a place of inquiry and concern. If graduates from our public schools are thinking in these exclusivist and racist ways, then why is school so important? What knowledge are we actually communicating and cultivating each day?

Reflecting on my father's question and my inability to immediately respond to his probe sparked a personal epiphany. Skyrocketing graduation rates, more participation in co-curricular opportunities, increased diversity and achievement in higher-level courses, and increased test scores, were indicators of academic achievement. However, academic achievement means nothing if our graduates are not inspired to be better, more loving people.

Therefore, I issue a challenge:

1. Choose to cultivate a LOVING Culture in all of your schools and classrooms

Developing a Culture of Love requires inclusive and forgiving policies, the transformative teaching and learning practices to meet the need of each contemporary learner, and uncomfortable conversations about systems in need of change. Continue to appreciate that great individuals do not transform culture, but instead great teams lead sustainable change efforts.

2. Mentor and support an aspiring school leader

The percentage of superintendents in New York state expecting to retire in the next three years is 63% (Snapshot, 2015). The education profession is experiencing a leadership crisis. Cultivating loving cultures in schools requires creative, committed, and knowledgeable leaders now and into the future. We must recruit, inspire, and encourage talented individuals to pursue school leadership roles. The next generation of leaders must be representative of the great diversity that exists amongst our students. For this reason, I also ask that those reading this book strive to encourage and support women and people of color as they seek leadership positions.

141

Hopefully, my children, Aiden and Landyn, will one day have opportunities to lead successful organizations. I dream that said organizations will reflect the rich diversity that makes our nation great. More specifically, when my children become adult leaders, I wish for the discourse surrounding public education to be devoid of negativity related to politics, funding, and poor student achievement. Instead, I pray that conversations dominating the public education landscape will be about continuously improving the Culture of Love that exists in each one of our classrooms and schools. A Culture of Love in public education has been transformative for me, my family, and my school community. Let's make sure that this vision becomes so for all.

CHAPTER TWENTY-NINE

OUR WORK IS NEVER DONE

Establishing a Culture of Love is hard work. The only thing harder is sustaining it. As time passes, people sitting in board of education and superintendent seats transition. Teachers move on and students graduate.

> *Organizations improve in direct proportion to the amount of conflict it can maintain. #CultureofLove*

The organizational ethos should not change however as various personalities changeover. Instead, a Culture of Love becomes more deeply embedded when leaders in an organization continue to focus on the following things:

STAYING GREAT

A commitment to continuous improvement

In February 2016, I shared the Water Authority's water test results with our school community. The news was alarming as the tests revealed high levels of lead in our schools' drinking water. Water samplings from sinks and drinking fountains throughout our district showed lead levels that exceeded the action level established by the Environmental Protection Agency (EPA). Along with this troubling data, folks' frustration was compounded as communication breakdowns had led to delayed notification of action level exceedances.

At a community meeting created to share more details about the troubling data, a concerned mother asked, "Dr. Brown, do we truly have a Culture of Love when we make mistakes and miss things like this?" I responded with, "Yes. If you are looking for weaknesses and mistakes in our organization, you will find them. But we are all in control of whether or not those issues impede our work." I went on to affirm that the water quality issues and associated communication gaps were the result of absent or broken organizational systems. After acknowledging the mistakes, I mentioned a few other areas also in need of improvement in our school district.

A Culture of Love is needed and most apparent when things don't go well. Trust, commitment, and patience are essential in navigating complex issues facing our school district and community. When exhibiting loving behaviors, a positive and constructive culture is ever present, regardless of the magnitude of an emerging situation.

At the contentious community meeting about water quality, I explained, "Every time we recognize and correct a broken system, there will be at least ten more that require our attention." A healthy and loving culture requires continuous improvement and the ongoing identification and recognition of areas that need to be fixed. It is important to note small wins and current successes, however, to maintain a Culture of Love, leaders need to constantly ask, "How do we get better tomorrow?" In a Culture of Love, folks are building for the long term, while doing their best today.

Letting go of being *right*

To continuously improve in a Culture of Love, leaders need to spend more time asking great questions and less time providing answers. Ongoing inquiry and commitment to learning happen best when leaders express humility and resist the need to always be right. Solving problems, new discoveries, and forging strong coalitions require multiple perspectives. No one point of view is always correct, and frankly all viewpoints can be shifted by new information and thinking. When leaders let go of their egos and the need to be right, constructive cooperation increases and destructive competition decreases.

Don't be concerned with who gets the credit

In a Culture of Love, successes lead to more success. When breakthroughs and accomplishments occur, it is important to note the team's contributions. In

Ithaca, we do much to recognize the many ways students and staff achieve. An example of our celebration of achievement is the quarterly commendations ceremonies hosted by the board of education. At these special ceremonies, board members and I recognize academic and athletic accomplishments, extraordinary community service, and other special achievements. As we shake the hands of National Merit Finalists, Eagle Scouts, State Champions, Master Teachers, and others we are further defining what excellence means in our organization.

At each of the commendations ceremonies, when sharing thoughts in district publications, and during media interviews I am purposeful with my use of the words "We" and the "District". In a Culture of Love, we achieve together, we struggle together, we fail together, and we learn together. Every individual in our organization is part of the "District". Therefore, when referencing the "District" one should not be referencing an individual leader, an authority figure, or a governing body. The "District" is all of us together.

CHAPTER THIRTY

THE PRIVATE SECTOR

My experiences cultivating a Culture of Love took place in public institutions. However, the philosophies and actions presented in this book are transferable to leaders and entities operating in private settings as well. Recruiting and developing people, determining key levers that contribute to organizational aspirations, and establishing accountability metrics that align with the vision and mission are examples of culture building strategies needed in all organizations.

An approach to continuous improvement, brings like challenges both in the public and private sectors. Issues such as transitioning the prevailing internal sentiment from *Them* to *Us* and shifting the focus from individuals to teams requires strong leadership regardless of the type of organization. Additionally, great leaders in any organization encourage self-reflection, constructive conflict, and needed policy shifts. When reviewing the tactics described in this book, a leader in the private sector may seek to exchange

> *People in a healthy organization learn from one another, confront serious issues, and recover quickly from mistakes.*
> *#CultureofLove*

terms like *student* and *school district* with *customer* and *business.*

A deeply embedded collaborative culture is only possible when leaders evaluate their own behaviors and reflect on their personal contributions to the vision, mission, and culture the organization seeks to build. I often say that institutions are perfectly constructed to produce the results they are getting. In other words, meaningful change is only possible when policies and systems are reformed. This is not easy to do as it requires individuals to self-assess and change long-standing behaviors

Leaders in public and private establishments must expend the time and effort necessary to recognize their compliance and engagement within various systems. For example, organizations seeking to transform behaviors and policies with the purpose of becoming more diverse and inclusive must start with an investigation of their current state. With a deep understanding of existing issues, folks can better tailor solutions. Leaders can then begin the self-reflection process by engineering an opportunity for all employees to respond to questions like:

- What is implicit and explicit bias, and how is it influencing our organization?

- How does bias show up in employee behavior? Or in the decisions we make and how we treat people?
- How do we mitigate that behavior?

One Fortune 500 company with over 125,000 workers, has committed to always thinking about how they might be more inclusive and to making sure there aren't any hidden biases impacting the organization's thinking. This private pharmaceutical company used results from surveys and other reflection methods to inform the development of a dynamic website that helps employees understand the benefits of working collaboratively in groups that are more diverse.

Likewise, one of the world's largest communications and entertainment companies is experiencing success with diversity and inclusion initiatives after spending significant time reviewing behaviors and policies. This company has created a dozen Employee Resource Groups (ERG) and Employee Networks (EN). An ERG provides support, advocacy, education, mentoring, and more to women, military veterans, people with disabilities, and members of the LGBTQ community. An EN is an informal group that focusses on professional development by using cross-functional and diverse teams.

These diversity and inclusion initiatives take place within successful companies that exhibit a relentless approach to establishing a positive and healthy organizational culture. Private companies with such commitment attract and retain the best talent in the industry. The same is true for school districts and other public institutions. This Culture of Love encourages diversity, inclusion, open communication, and mentoring across genders and ethnicities, and support for employees' socio-emotional health. The best people want to work in places like this!

Such talented individuals contribute to more-and-more organizational success. Achievements in public institutions have significant community-wide impact on social, political, and economic structures. Likewise, successful cultivation of a Culture of Love in the private sector adds to the overall common good. Specifically, movements to be more inclusive and culturally responsive contribute to social justice, thus having implications far beyond the company's walls. As both private businesses and public institutions become more welcoming and responsive to all people, a healthy community-wide ethos becomes deeply entrenched and sustainable.

CHAPTER THIRTY-ONE

WHAT'S NEXT?

In the spring of 2015, a team of educators from Chicago came and spent the day in one of the ICSD's middle schools. These secondary school educators from the Chicago Public School District, one of the largest in the nation, had heard of the restorative practices being used in Ithaca. They were particularly interested in how a middle school might operate without a traditional In-School Suspension program.

After spending hours in classrooms observing and interviewing teachers, the Chicago-based team of educators was inspired to return to their district armed

> *Leaders fulfill today's expectations and define the future agenda.*
> *#CultureofLove*

with new philosophies and practical strategies to experiment within their respective schools. The visitors paid special attention to the reflection strategies used with all students, the alternatives to suspension offered, and the various other interventions in place for students.

Ironically however, though initially most interested in alternatives to discipline, when debriefing their visit, restorative practices had not been the only impactful strategy observed during their time in Ithaca. Instead, the Chicago educators left Ithaca radically inspired by a group of sixth graders highly engaged in physical education.

That day, the students were focused on developing their badminton skills, and were observed learning and tracking their individual progress using their school-provided mobile devices. The Chicago educators went on to share other examples of high-yield instructional strategies being used to engage students in Ithaca. They also raved about all the many positive relationships they had observed between the students and adults throughout the building.

Reaction from the Chicago team is not unlike that acknowledged from other guests who often converge on our city. Educators frequently come to witness for themselves what has been described as a, "Remarkable story of transformation." By the time this book went to publication, the ICSD had attracted several hundred visitors from all over the world.

Educators come to observe and have conversations related to the implementation and artifacts associated with transdisciplinary curriculum, mobile technology device usage, enhanced co-curricular offerings, graduation coaching, restorative practices, and more. Along with gaining insights into best practices, visitors leave Ithaca filled with excitement and inspired by stories about our organizational culture. Visitors note that from the moment they arrive in our city, they are greeted with, and surrounded by, love. Friends recognize the fond way those who are part of our loving culture refer to the children, the organization, and the work we are attempting to accomplish together. The exuberance of love and pride even emanates from customer service representatives at the airport, in the hotels, and local restaurants. Visitors also note how instructional and non-instructional ICSD staff enthusiastically share their favorite mission moments.

School districts are typically a community's largest employer. While impacting many families personally and professionally, a school district provides a public model for the heart, spirit, and the philosophy of an entire geographic area. Other large employers can have similar impacts on a community too. With such influence comes much responsibility which is why I insist that cultivating a positive organizational culture is a primary responsibility of all organizations both public and private.

To further enhance community building, more public-private partnerships need to be established for the purpose of sharing resources and thinking. More importantly these mutually beneficial connections are needed to expand a positive and loving culture beyond the world of work and into our daily lives.

Artificial intelligence, sophisticated data mining software, and other emerging technologies continue to revolutionize economies through innovation and automation. Soon, employers will no longer require the same worker skills as before. The human ability to love is needed to compensate for the limitations of emerging technologies. As human work transitions from hands to hearts, the ability to love and think with others becomes increasingly valuable to an organization's survival in the global community. This love economy values a person's ability to build and maintain relationships through trust, patience, and forgiveness. Our communities must come together to ensure all citizens acquire loving skills and opportunities with which to construct their future.

I believe the community, students, and staff that comprise the Culture of Love in Ithaca, represent an important shift in leadership where school districts and other organizations are concerned. We are all leaders and our leadership must transcend the place where we work. Together, we must commit to establishing relationships and exhibiting the necessary personal humility needed to contribute to a community's evolution.

Cultivating a Culture of Love must be an essential part of all leaders' daily lives. Sustaining a healthy organizational culture and spreading the philosophy to other communities requires me and other leaders to constantly challenge ourselves. A loving culture requires continuous improvement. There is no end to the work and the journey is ongoing. Therefore, leaders need to constantly reflect on their behavior to determine areas where we are succeeding and those where additional focus is needed.

Continuous improvement further prompts new and enhanced strategies for teaching and learning. These innovations are joined by efforts to be more inviting to all members of our community. More inclusive and culturally responsive organizations are our best hope in eradicating various forms of oppression. Anti-marginalization practices are made possible through the attainment of academic and social skills needed to advocate for issues of social justice. The resulting reflections, conflict, and policy changes lead to shifts in access to housing, jobs, education, and other resources that have traditionally been more challenging for some people to access than for others. This must become a major, long term aspect of all organizational missions.

In school districts, a loving culture as described in this book inevitably leads to more student and adult activism. As school leaders embrace this activism, we must also take steps to develop the necessary skills within students and adults so they too can one day govern. In a Culture of Love, we are empowering one another to challenge existing systems, and at the same time, we are providing tools for others to become leaders in those same institutions. The mindset and strategies used to cultivate a Culture of Love are transferable to any school district, governmental agency, business, and more.

Equipped with inclusive education, social media, and other contemporaneous tools, the world's greatest generation of activists is currently sitting in classrooms. These young people can communicate with a worldwide audience of other empowered learners as they challenge and question the heads of small and large institutions and increasingly, entire nations. Now more than ever, leadership is needed to harness the energy necessary for political activism and to infuse it into new governance structures. Activism that is unparalleled to anything we've seen before, coupled with an understanding of how to build a positive and collaborative culture, leads to a new approach in governance. With love at its origin and operational core, the positive possibilities are infinite!

REFERENCES

Chingos, M. M., Whitehurst, G. J. R., & Lindquist, K. M. (2014). School superintendents: Vital or irrelevant. *Brown Center on Education Policy at Brookings.*

Clifton, D. O. (2005). *How full is your bucket? Positive strategies for work and life.* Gallup Press.

Collins, J. C., & Collins, J. (2001). *Good to great: Why some companies make the leap... and others don't.* Random House.

Darling-Hammond, L. (2015). *The flat world and education: How America's commitment to equity will determine our future.* Teachers College Press.

https://www.khanacademy.org/

https://mosbowsmemphis.com/pages/store-categories

Levin, B. (2000). Putting students at the center in education reform. *Journal of Educational Change, 1*(2), 155-172.

Manby, Joel (2012). LOVE Works: Seven Timeless Principles for Effective Leaders

Mullick, N. (2012). Caine's arcade. *Documentary.*

Schlechty, P. C. (2011). *Engaging students: The next level of working on the work.* John Wiley & Sons.

Snapshot 2015. The Council of School Superintendents: The 9th Triennial Study of the Superintendency in New York.

ABOUT THE AUTHOR

Luvelle Brown is an experienced educator who has held positions as teacher, assistant principal, principal, school CIO, and superintendent of schools. Dr. Brown is currently serving as Superintendent of the Ithaca City School District (ICSD) in Ithaca, NY. During his tenure there, the ICSD has experienced unprecedented levels of success.

Dr. Brown has facilitated conversations in multiple communities resulting in transformative shifts in culture and achievement. Using systems thinking in schools, Dr. Brown's leadership has led to innovative programs, redesigned learning spaces, and numerous technological initiatives.

He has received various awards and recognitions including: The 2017 New York State Superintendent of the Year as one of the nation's top educators and thought leaders (TrustED). Dr. Brown has also been recognized by the National School Boards' Association as a "20-to-Watch" and "Difference Maker", receiving the Center for Digital Education Top 30 Award, and the 2014 eSchool News Tech-Savvy Superintendent Award.

He was selected by the US Department of Education as one of the nation's top 100 Innovative Superintendents and was invited to be a featured speaker at President Barack Obama's 1st National Superintendent Summit at the White House. Additionally, Dr. Brown has served on the New York State Council of School Superintendents' (NYSCOSS) Executive Committee, The School Superintendents' Association (AASA) Digital Consortium, The Center for Digital Education Advisory Council, and CoSN's Empowered Superintendent Advisory Panel.

After attending Fluvanna County High School in Central Virginia, Dr. Brown went on to be one of the most decorated students in the history of the University of Virginia. He earned a Bachelor's of Science, a Masters of Teaching, Education Specialist, and an Education Doctorate from one of the nation's top universities. Currently, Dr. Brown serves as an adjunct faculty member at SUNY Cortland and St. John Fisher College.

An active community member through service on various non-profit boards, he was elected as a term Trustee at Ithaca College in the Spring of 2018. Additionally, Dr. Brown is a proud member of Kappa

Alpha Psi Fraternity, Inc. and is co-founder of the nationally recognized 100 Black Men of Central Virginia.

Luvelle Brown is a highly regarded speaker and workshop facilitator addressing a wide range of topics for local, regional, and national audiences. He has published numerous articles, the author of Culture of Love: Cultivating a Transformative and Positive Organizational Culture and the co-author of ThinkTweets: 100 Transformative Tweets for Educators. For more information or to book Dr. Brown for speaking engagements visit: www.LuvelleBrown.com

"Dr. Luvelle Brown possesses all the essential leadership gifts and readily displays them in this thought provoking work. **A Culture of Love: Cultivating Positive and Transformative School Culture***, speaks to the leadership gift of authorship- helping others paint their own canvass- putting their signature on it. It speaks to the leadership gift of empowerment- enabling others to feel the difference. And, it profoundly speaks to the gift of love- care and compassion lending to a sense of significance, finding meaning in contribution."*

Dr. L. Oliver Robinson.
Superintendent of Schools
Shenendehowa Central School District
2013 New York State Superintendent of the Year

"Dr. Brown has shifted the hearts and minds of our community to accept new ideas in public education through his inspirational leadership. He is a visionary leader that effects positive change in our children's lives."

Brenda Prince
President, Ithaca Parent Teacher Association Council

"Dr. Brown has an unwavering commitment to equity and inclusion in education. His leadership has resulted in my personal and professional growth. I am so profoundly grateful that he has created an organizational culture where student and adult thinking and learning are welcomed and encouraged."

Alexandra Spencer

Teacher, Ithaca City School District

"Luvelle Brown emulates the characteristics of a strong, educational leader. Most important are his efforts to advocate for children, public education, and to provide equity and access for all students. To do this successfully Dr. Brown models appropriate social and emotional awareness, focused listening skills, promotes the use of technology as a learning tool, welcomes active participation, and works collaboratively with those who provide services in the District."

Susan Mittler

New York State Board of Regents

6th Judicial District